A People's History of Walthamstow

A People's History of
Walthamstow

James Diamond

First published 2018

The History Press
The Mill, Brimscombe Port
Stroud, Gloucestershire, GL5 2QG
www.thehistorypress.co.uk

British Library Cataloguing in Publication Data.
A catalogue record for this book is available from the British Library.

ISBN 978 0 7509 7899 6

Typesetting and origination by The History Press
Printed in Great Britain

Contents

Acknowledgements

My main thanks are to Steve Gardner and Jo Parker at Waltham Forest Archives and Local Studies Library, who have helped me every step of the way with their detailed knowledge of the area and sources at Vestry House. I would like to thank Bill George at the Essex Field Club for providing biographical information and images, and Helen Hawkins at Pre-Construct Archaeology for giving more background about the 2017 excavation at Vinegar Alley, and other archaeological sites in the area. Oona Kelly at Walthamstow School for Girls provided very useful details about the building of the Greek Theatre. Alistair MacLellan allowed me to use his information about German shopkeepers on the eve of the Great War. I would also like to thank the archivists at the Salvation Army Heritage Centre, and the Co-operative Society Archives for the help they have given. St Mary's Church kindly allowed me to photograph the Monoux brasses and Merry monument. I would also like to thank the staff at Essex Record Office for their help.

Lastly, thanks to Kim Gladwin for reading drafts of the chapters and being so supportive throughout the writing of this book.

Introduction: Beating the Bounds

Where is Walthamstow? Most people know it's the last stop on the Victoria line of the Tube or that it is somewhere amid the sprawl of suburbs in north-east London. But knowing exactly where it stops and another area starts is trickier, even for the people who live there.

That wasn't always so. For centuries a custom was performed in Walthamstow and many other rural communities called beating the bounds, in which people walked around their parish boundaries to remind them where they lay and check that neighbouring communities hadn't encroached. Those taking part in the perambulation in the days before a detailed map existed followed hedges, trees and marker posts and relied on whatever knowledge was in the heads of the community's oldest members.

One of the last beating of the bounds took place in June 1951 as part of the then borough's celebration of the Festival of Britain and was organised as a good-humoured revival by the Walthamstow Antiquarian Society. The custom hadn't been performed since 1867 when around 200 people, accompanied by a fife and drum band and bell-ringers, walked around the borders of what was a quiet parish in a largely rural corner of Essex. By 1951 things were a little different. The participants were driven parts of the way in a coach and two school buses around what had become a dormitory suburb of London, which was famous across Britain as the home of the artist William Morris and a greyhound-racing track.

In 1951 the party of schoolchildren and local history enthusiasts started at Whipps Cross at a spot near Walthamstow's boundary with Woodford and Wanstead, where they put down a portable cardboard marker brought along for the occasion. The old ways were kept up. The schoolchildren carried willow wands and a coach horn – as the parishioners had done in 1867 – and symbolically 'beat' the ground with the wands around the marker post and blew the instrument to confirm where one of the ancient bounds lay. Two of the schoolboys, who were unsure of the boundary, were tamely 'bumped', thrown up and down by the children, and presented with a penny by the other beaters to help them remember, exactly as they would have been in the old days.

They then followed Walthamstow's boundary – marked out by the Woodford New Road – to the Napier Arms, where they split into two groups to complete the circuit. One group, led by Frank Maynard, whose family had a long connection with Walthamstow going back many generations, took a trolleybus down Lea Bridge Road to follow the southern boundary with Leyton to the Walthamstow marshes. The larger group walked along Sunset Avenue through a remnant of forest and took the coach northwards up Hatch Lane and Larkshall Road to Rolls Cottage at Chingford Hatch, where they beat the bounds again with their wands around the cardboard post. This was Walthamstow's northernmost boundary. As the older members watched from the vehicles, a group of beaters carried their willow wands westwards through the grounds of the British Xylonite Factory and strode along Higham Station Avenue. This area had been an isolated rural community known as Hale End until the Victorians built the railway and called the station Highams Park. The beaters continued on foot, crossing the River Ching at Chapel End and walking to Higham Hill to meet the coach at Folly Lane and beat the bounds again. They then walked up Cooper Avenue, one of the highest points in the area, from where they could look out over the water reservoirs and towards Middlesex. They then took the coach to the Ferry Boat Inn, which stood close to the River Lea, which had always been Walthamstow's historic boundary with Tottenham, where they met Frank Maynard's party and the Mayor and Mayoress of Walthamstow for tea.

After the cakes and sandwiches the schoolchildren, carrying their willow wands, and members of Walthamstow Antiquarian Society clambered back into the vehicles. They drove down Blackhorse Road and crossed Coppermill Lane near the High Street. The coaches and buses headed down Markhouse Road past the rows of brick housing built in the nineteenth century, which mushroomed after the railway to Walthamstow opened in 1870. Then they turned into the long straight Boundary Road, the border with the borough of Leyton, before driving back to the spot in Whipps Cross where they had started.

Schoolchildren beat the bounds outside the Ferry Boat Inn, June 1951. (Courtesy of Vestry House Museum, London Borough of Waltham Forest)

Walking around is still a good way to learn about Walthamstow's history and the people who have lived there. There's the olde worlde bits the Victorians first started to put on postcards: the Ancient House, Monoux almshouses and St Mary's Church. But even spotting a builder's monograph on a house in Chapel End, a faded advert on a wall for an Edwardian grocery in St James Street, or a Victorian shop sign lurking beneath a modern façade in the High Street will reveal something interesting. Just strolling around, even if it's not around the boundaries, is a good place to begin.

James Diamond, 2018

A Note on Spellings and Figures

There are many variant spellings of places and place names in Walthamstow. I chose to use Joseph Jeffreys for the person and Jeffries for the square. St James Street is also spelt with the possessive, but not in all sources and I have stuck to that form without the possessive. Not all spellings have been modernised and were spelt out as they appeared in the original source, so Marsh Street was Mershe Strete.

Pounds, shillings and pence also appear with the abbreviations *l*, *s*, *d*. as they do in the sources.

Abbreviations

BM	British Museum
ERO	Essex Record Office
LMA	London Metropolitan Archives
TNA	The National Archives
WFALSL	Waltham Forest Archives and Local Studies Library

1

Man and Mammoth: From the Ice Age to the Romans

In the late 1860s two scholars at the British Museum started to visit a spot in Walthamstow where gangs of navvies were digging up an area of meadowland. Dr Henry Woodward, a palaeontologist, and his colleague Augustus Wollaston Franks, the Keeper of British and Medieval Antiquities, were eager to discover what remains might have been preserved deep in the earth.

The workmen were excavating an enormous area of land near to the old course of the River Lea to build a chain of water reservoirs and filter beds for the East London Waterworks Company. Sifting through the mounds of peat and clay scooped out as the reservoirs were dug, Woodward discovered the bones of wild horses, wolves and beavers, extinct animals that had thrived in the forest which once covered the area. Amid the deepest deposits of gravel left over from the Ice Age, when glaciers had scraped out the river channel, he found the fossilised remains of a giant-antlered reindeer and the fragments of a mammoth's molar tooth and tusk.

That wasn't all. The two scholars also found human skulls and bones as well as bronze spearheads, a dagger handle and earthen pots that Franks catalogued as Celtic. Woodward dug a flint scraper out of a reservoir bank with his hands and by parleying with the workmen Franks acquired an armlet and a stag's horn club. Among the oldest Bronze Age pottery was a Deverel-Rimbury jar. Most of the pots were dated to the Iron Age and were thought to have been made by descendants of Celtic tribespeople who had migrated from the Continent and travelled along the Lea Valley.

Older artefacts have been discovered in Walthamstow. In the late nineteenth-century, Neolithic objects including hand axes were found in Higham Hill and around Hoe Street, and during the digging of the site for the borough's electricity generating station at Exeter Road workmen found a flint axe that has been dated at around 20,000 years old. There has been a human presence in the area since the Stone Age.

The evidence for the first human settlement is less clear. The fossil collector Dr Frank Corner claimed to have found a pile-dwelling settlement at one of the reservoirs in Walthamstow. Pile dwellings, also called 'crannogs', were wooden structures erected on the shores of lakes and rivers and there have been discoveries of Bronze Age pile dwellings in Ireland and Scotland and East Anglia. Dr Corner reported finding timber stakes about 4ft long driven into the sand and gravel, but a sketch was the only recording. There were also apparently the remnants of pile dwellings discovered on the right bank of the old River Lea during the excavation of the Banbury reservoir in 1900 or thereabouts.

In 2017, evidence of Iron Age settlement was identified by archaeologists excavating an area alongside Vinegar Alley near St Mary's Church. Discoveries at the site included a ring ditch, which might have encircled prehistoric dwellings, and quarrying pits. The topography of the area suited human settlement: it was a hillside capped with brick-earth, which would have been dug for pottery or building materials, and had a fertile, well-drained soil. Just as importantly, there was fresh water because springs would have bubbled up through the gravel strata offering a constant supply, and the Fillebrook stream flowed nearby. Strategically, it was a strongpoint with commanding views of the

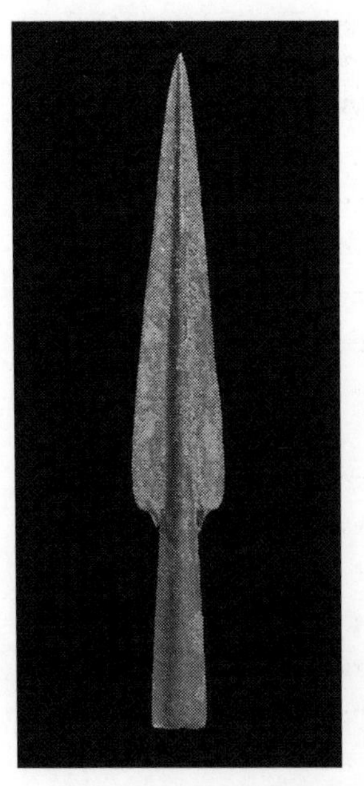

A Bronze Age spearhead discovered at the reservoirs in Walthamstow by Augustus Wollaston Franks. (© Trustees of the British Museum)

valley, and it protected homesteads from winter flooding. It wasn't the only Iron Age settlement in the Lea Valley. Other settlements were established as hill forts at Ambresbury Banks and Loughton Camp on the ridgeway in today's Epping Forest, although the Iron Age population of the entire Lea Valley was probably no more than 300 families or so.

Pathways would have linked Iron Age settlements and some of the footpaths walked by the Victorians probably followed the course of Iron Age routes. The Black Path, a name which suggests a thoroughfare worn down and trod by human feet over many centuries, was until the late nineteenth century the quickest route over the meadows from Walthamstow to a crossing point at the River Lea. Stretches can still be followed today.

The first people lived in a landscape of marshland and dense forests which were natural barriers to settlement. They cleared woodland, but draining the marshes along the River Lea would have required an engineering skill probably unknown to them, and their agriculture was probably small, square fields of crops. Wild grasses in the wetlands supported pastoral agriculture and the rearing of animals. In the deposits at the reservoir Henry Woodward discovered an abundance of goat bones and the remains of British cattle, an ancient small breed, suggesting that livestock was grazing on the river foreshore. They also fished. In 2016, at a site near what was the old course of the River Lea, archaeologists uncovered what was probably the wooden remains of a Bronze Age fish trap or fishing platform.

By the first century there was an increasing sophistication in agriculture as the Iron Age farmers started to use the ox-drawn mouldboard plough to turn the clay soils and south-east England even started to export wheat. The increasing wealth and resources attracted the Romans to England, who infiltrated into the Lea Valley. Again, the Romans would have travelled along the valley because it was the quickest route into the interior as the migrating Celtic tribes had done before them. But there was now a settled agricultural community of ancient British farmers who resisted them, and according to legend Boudica fought against the Roman armies from Loughton Camp and Ambresbury Banks.

However, archaeological discoveries in Walthamstow show that over many generations the settled community was integrated into Roman society. As well as Franks' earlier finds in 1903, Charles Hercules Read, a Keeper at the British Museum, excavated the pile dwelling site. He discovered what were probably wares from a river trade including Romano-British urns, jars, vessels and an iron knife as everyday Roman goods were used in households. He also found a Romano-British glass bead and a copper alloy trumpet brooch, suggesting that the people were adopting new styles of Roman-influenced dress.

Not all Romano-British objects found in Walthamstow have been domestic. Workmen dug up a bronze medal on a building site in Vallentin Road in 1931. The first-century token was given out as a souvenir for patrons of a circus. On one side there is the portrayal of a chariot race and on the reverse a dedication to a Roman man, presumably of high status, named Divus Nerva Traianus.

The settlement developed at the Vinegar Alley site during the Romano-British age. The 2017 excavation also uncovered, near to the ring ditch, a large Roman farmstead built within a boundary bank. The farmstead was most likely a collection of dwellings, made of timber and wattle and daub, with fields created by clearing the surrounding forest. A Roman coin and flue tiles were found, possibly indicating a high-status building with underfloor heating, or even a bathhouse in the countryside outside London.

The settlement wasn't isolated. As well as the river, a secondary Roman road ran along the nearby ridgeway leading up towards Epping Forest, following the course of what was probably an Iron Age path. The Romans also built a road to Colchester to the south-west of the Lea Valley and it's been suggested that the straight course of Boundary Road in Walthamstow follows the route of an old Roman road, which ran from a high point in the Essex countryside to London.

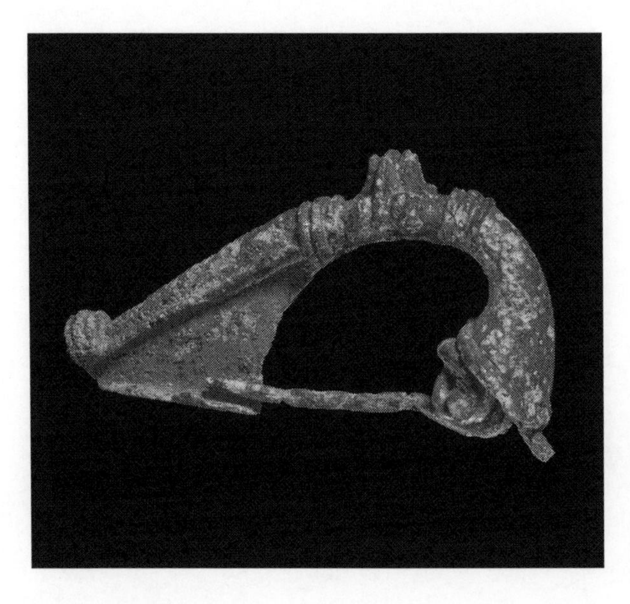

The Roman trumpet-brooch found in Walthamstow by Charles Hercules Read. (© Trustees of the British Museum)

By about the fifth century Romano-British society had withered across the Lea Valley. By then another Roman farmstead further up the valley at Sewardstone appears to have been abandoned, as had a villa and agricultural estate at Wanstead and another high-status building in Leyton, uncovered over a 2-acre site by workmen in 1718. The farmstead at Vinegar Alley was probably also deserted by then as well.

Over many centuries the area of what is now Walthamstow had from the Bronze Age felt the presence of migrating tribespeople and had been inhabited by Iron Age farmers. In the Romano-British age farmsteads were established and the area was linked to the wider world through a currency and trading system. But from the fifth century or so, after Romano-British society had collapsed, a new people were approaching who would transform the area and give it a name.

2

Wilcume's Place: Anglo-Saxon Walthamstow

It is likely that in the fifth century or so the first bands of people speaking a Germanic dialect started to wander into the Lea Valley, and they would have discovered that cultivation had faltered at the Romano-British farmsteads in the area.

These were Anglo-Saxon tribespeople who first settled on the eastern seaboard and migrated inland. Archaeologists are now sceptical of the idea that hordes of Saxons, Jutes and Angles invaded and drove out the native Britons, a popular theory among nineteenth-century antiquarians. The newcomers are likely to have arrived in dribs and drabs over many generations rather than in a mass migration, and there was co-existence and intermingling with the settled population.

There's material evidence from Walthamstow of the new cultures which were being introduced during this migration period. At the pile dwelling site, the British Museum's Charles Hercules Read found Anglo-Saxon jewellery, including two rings made of twisted copper alloy wire made in the sixth century. Read also found a bird brooch, which is thought to have been Merovingian in origin, from the Frankish rulers of northern Europe. It is a fine piece of craftsmanship: the sixth-century brooch has a hooked beak with a garnet inlaid as an eye, and a tail set with a garnet. Normally, Merovingian

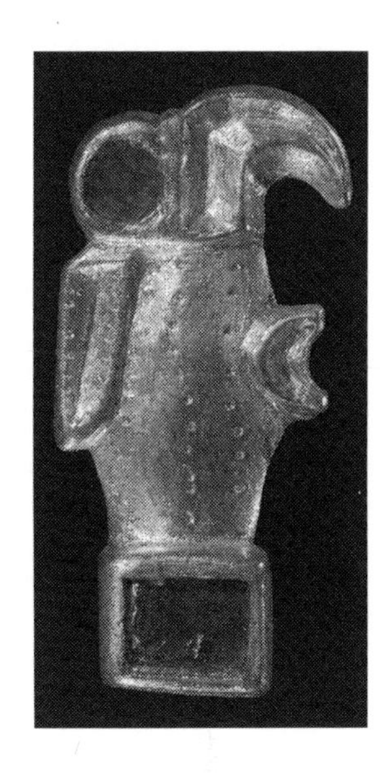

The sixth-century bird brooch found by Charles Hercules Read in Walthamstow. (© Trustees of the British Museum)

women wore a tunic covered with a cloak, which was fastened in place with one or two brooches. The brooch and rings suggest the assimilation of Anglo-Saxon or Frankish culture, or incomers travelling along the valley routes.

The strongest evidence for Anglo-Saxon settlement in the Walthamstow area is place names. Over generations the people of the area started to speak Old English, a new language which amalgamated Frisian and Germanic dialects with a smattering of British and Latin words. Old English names for features in the landscape survive in Walthamstow today. A ridge was a landmark in the landscape and in Old English the people used the word *hoh* to describe the rise of ground. The description is the origin of Hoe Street, the course of which still follows a spur of ground.

They also named their settlements. Today's Higham Hill stems from *Heah-ham*, combining the Old English *heah* – meaning something lofty or tall – with *ham* for homestead. The Anglo-Saxons also used personal names to describe a settlement. On the high ground across the valley from the hill at *Heah-ham* was *Totta's-ham* or the homestead of an Anglo-Saxon man named Totta. Further up the valley there was a place called *Sigeweard's-tun* (a *tun* was an enclosed dwelling or homestead) after an Anglo-Saxon named Sigweard who established it. Today, it is the hamlet of Sewardstone.

About this time, the place name emerged which evolved over the centuries into today's modern spelling of Walthamstow. So was Walthamstow a personal place name in origin as well? The favoured explanation is that travellers reaching the settlement who had walked through the dense forests used the word *wilcume*, meaning welcome, and *stow* for place, to describe the attractiveness of the area – it was the 'welcome-place'. However, Wilcume was certainly an Anglo-Saxon female name and it's known that there was a queen and an abbess named Wilcume as well as ordinary women with the name. Furthermore, it wasn't unusual for an important woman in Anglo-Saxon society to have her name attached to a settlement and women did own land. In Cambridgeshire is the village of Wilburton, which evolved from *Wilburg's-tun*, named after an Anglo-Saxon woman.

So there could have been a local woman named Wilcume who was the origin of the place name. In Old English *stow* meant 'a locality' and 'a place which is built', but place names with the Old English word *stow* are also often associated with meeting places for worship. While there is no written record of a Wilcume in the area, it's possible there was an important woman who was linked to a religious meeting place. By the seventh century East Saxons had adopted Christianity so the origins of the place name *Wilcume's-stow* might go back to that conversion period. Victorian antiquarians liked to believe that present-day St Mary's Church was on the site of an earlier Saxon church.

What is certain is that the place name was spoken and passed down for many generations by local people before it was ever formally recorded or written down. Anglo-Saxon society was one of mass illiteracy in which knowledge of place names was circulated by word-of-mouth, at first in the immediate area to identify a particular settlement and then, gradually, it spread outside the locality.

So what did the Anglo-Saxon settlements look like? They were originally probably just a scattering of farmsteads or homesteads in which people of the same kinship group lived. They were made up of granaries, outbuildings, animal enclosures and workshops, as well as rectangular wood-framed dwellings with thatched roofs. To create fields, they worked outwards, cutting down the encircling forest. Their cattle and pigs grazed on the seedlings in the undergrowth, thus stopping the regeneration of the woodland. There's no archaeological evidence in today's Walthamstow, as yet, of where Anglo-Saxon settlements might have been located. A natural spot was the Vinegar Alley site; however, no remains from as late as the fifth to sixth centuries were found in 2017. But dwellings in the early Anglo-Saxon period were built in wood and goods were made of textiles and leather, so they are less likely to have survived the centuries.

However, more evidence of people living in the area during the Anglo-Saxon period has been found near the old River Lea. In 1900, labourers digging up Mitchley Marsh to build the reservoirs discovered a 15ft-long dugout boat hewn from a trunk of oak and, lying inside, was a punting pole. The craft had probably been tethered to a bank and swept away. In 1901 members of the Essex Field Club who inspected the boat, which had been stored away in a shed at the reservoirs, believed it was prehistoric. But recent carbon dating shows the oak was felled in the local forests between the seventh and ninth century. Dugout boats have also been found at Sewardstone and further downstream of the River Lea at Clapton. They

A drawing of the dugout Anglo-Saxon boat discovered at Lockwood Reservoir. (Courtesy of the Essex Field Club)

were used for trading and fishing on the river and as a way of travelling between the settlements throughout the Anglo-Saxon period.

The Saxons' most useful tool was a *sax* or *scramasax*, a short-bladed knife, which was so important that they named themselves in its honour. An iron *scramasax* dating from the ninth or tenth century was also found at the Walthamstow reservoirs. The knife was a practical tool, but also a weapon. By the ninth century, the local people must have felt threatened by harrying campaigns as Scandinavian invaders were starting to approach their area.

Ninth-century spearheads and swords, discovered around the old course of the Lea, are evidence of fighting in the area when the Scandinavians fought the Anglo-Saxon kingdoms led by King Alfred. In the ninth century a chunk of territory was ceded to the Scandinavians by treaty, which used the River Lea as a boundary to mark the Danelaw. Yet it's unlikely that Scandinavian occupation extended over the communities at *Wilcume's-stow*, as the place names of Scandinavian origin in today's Essex are mainly clustered along the coast.

Vikings still became part of local legend. It is known that Viking ships travelled up the River Lea during their campaigns against King Alfred. When a sword, skeleton remains and a clinker-built boat were found in Mitchley Marsh in 1900 during the construction of the Lockwood Reservoir, it was thought to be a Viking craft, largely thanks to overheated newspaper speculation. Even some members of the Essex Field Club, who inspected the craft, thought it was Scandinavian and archaeological records later recorded it as a ship burial. Only in the 1970s, when fragments of the vessel's wooden planking were carbon dated, was the vessel established as most likely to have been a seventeenth-century river barge.

By the eleventh century the settlements had evolved into communities of 200 or so people at *Wilcume's-stow* and on the hilltop at *Heah-ham*. From

The craft discovered near the old course of the River Lea in 1900. (Courtesy of London Metropolitan Archives. Permission of Thames Water)

their scattered farmsteads the people were gradually enclosing more forest and ploughing larger fields. They had pasture for their sheep and cattle and meadows. Every year in the late summer, they marked Lammas Day, meaning *hláf-mæsse* or 'bread-mass', and the word 'lammas' was still used in Walthamstow in the nineteenth century to describe the rights to graze livestock on the meadows near the River Lea.

These societies were organised in a manorial system. No Old English charters have survived to show the boundaries of the manor of *Wilcume's-stow*, but a charter from 1062 for the neighbouring manor of *Wudeforde*, or Woodford, states that its bounds included the River Ching, which it called Angrice's *burne* or stream. The Ching must have been one boundary of *Wilcume's-stow*, or *Wilcumestow* as some may have called it, with the marshlands to the south, the River Lea and the forest providing other natural boundaries. The manorial system organised a hierarchical community: the estate was owned by a tenant-in-chief, who was largely absent, and managed by manorial officials day-to-day. There was a peasantry of villagers and smallholders and at the very bottom were slaves.

Under the last Anglo-Saxon kings, the people of these areas were part of a large administrative unit called a Hundred. The leading residents would have travelled to Becontree Heath near Dagenham to take part in a moot, or assembly, for the Becontree Hundred in the shire of Essex to discuss local affairs. In 1066 there must have been talk of just one event: a new invader had arrived and slain the Anglo-Saxon king of England. The Norman Conquest would overturn their society and even in the manors near the River Lea, people's lives would be changed forever.

3

Villeins and Villages: Life in the Medieval Manors

A glimpse of the ordinary people of Walthamstow's manors appears in the folios of a national survey completed in 1086 which the people in later centuries called Domesday, Old English for doomsday, because like the Judgement Day they thought its decision was final and could not be overturned.

Domesday Book has a folio for the manor of Wilcumestou, a Latinised version of the Old English place name, which reveals that a Norman-named Countess Judith was the tenant-in-chief in 1086 but, before the Conquest, it has been just one estate among many owned by Waltheof. He was a powerful Anglo-Saxon earl with landholdings across the north of England and East Anglia who had kept his lands in 1066, but was compelled to marry Judith, a niece of the new king. In 1076 he was executed after supporting a revolt against King William, and Judith was given his land.

Wilcumestou was valuable. In 1086 there were ten and a half hides of land (a hide was 120 acres), pasture worth 8*s* rent and 80 acres of meadow. There was also a watermill, which probably stood on today's Copper Mill Stream. The demesne, a separate farm or area of land owned by the tenant-in-chief, had eight cattle, twenty-five goats, thirty-five pigs, sixty sheep and one cob, a horse from Normandy. By 1086 the manor was worth £28 and 2oz of gold.

The manor's population rose after the Norman Conquest. Domesday records the people in 1066 and in 1086 as 'then 25 *villeins*; now 36, then 1 bordar now 25; always 4 slaves'. Only heads of households were counted, so, by 1086, there was a population of about 270 people. All were unfree peasants. A *villein* was a rent-paying peasant who had a farmstead but owed labour duties to the manor, while a *bordar* was of lower status and had more onerous labour obligations, especially at harvest, and usually lived in a cottage smallholding. Slaves only toiled on the demesne, often as a ploughmen. Two slaves worked each plough: one guided the oxen as the other directed the plough, turning the soil.

Hecham, Domesday's version of *Heah-ham*, was a far smaller manor. Domesday records that there were 'then 8 *villeins*, now 10; then 2 bordars now 3, always 4 slaves'. A free man named Halfdan held five hides in 1066. Free men were independent farmers who worked their own land, but there were few in Essex as they tended to be in the old Danelaw areas. At Hecham, two other free men had held one hide. By 1086, a Norman named Peter de Valognes, a standard-bearer at Hastings, had displaced Halfdan and annexed the other free men's hide to his estate and installed a Norman subtenant on the land.

The large rise in population at Wilcumestou was because *bordar* families were settled from outside the manor to clear woodland. By 1086 the manor had woodland for 300 pigs, the same as Hecham, suggesting that there had been extensive clearance of the old forested area. There were fifteen men's ploughs at the Conquest, and twenty-two by 1086, so the area of arable farming land had grown considerably in a generation as fields were extended by 'assarting', the act of enclosing the forest and then breaking up the ground for tillage. At Hecham the three *bordar* families may have been the households of Halfdan and the two other free men from 1066, who had been dispossessed of their land.

Domesday Book recorded the complaint of Peter de Valognes after he acquired Haldane's demesne farm on which 'he found nothing except one ox and one acre sown'. It was valued at 60*s*. The demesne was developed rapidly. By 1086, there was '15 cattle, 1 cob, 37 pigs and 2 beehives' (the peasants' livestock wasn't counted) and valued at £4 10*s*. *Villeins* and *bordars* would have been put to work on the demesne, shepherding and feeding the livestock, harvesting the crops and beekeeping, which was a lucrative industry as honey was so valuable that rents could be paid in it.

Wilcumestou remained the property of a Norman family for many years. Ralph de Toni, whose father had fought at the Battle of Hastings, acquired the manor after he married a daughter of Judith and Waltheof named Alice and renamed it Walthamstow Toni. One of his most important decisions was to build a manorial church on the hilltop where St Mary's Church stands today. After his death in about 1108, Alice awarded the church with lands to the Holy Trinity Priory of Aldgate for the souls of her late husband and her dead son, Hugh.

The church was the most important building in the manor. Over generations the Norman manorial church was extended and rebuilt and a bell tower was added as it became a medieval parish church dedicated to the Virgin Mary. But the church was for more than religious observance. St Mary the Virgin was the only public building in the parish and the south porch, where the laity entered, is thought to have been used for discussing secular business and affairs of the parish and would have been a meeting place for parish guilds as well.

The importance the church played in people's lives can be seen in the gifts which people left in their wills, such as Matilda Webbe who, in 1426, left a sheep to the high altar and money for repairs to the font, while in 1431 Richard Feis left a book to the altar. Others gave money and livestock for repairs and works. But the most popular bequest was to the lights of the church, which were candles and oil lamps standing next to religious images or objects of significance for worshippers. In 1491 a labourer named Richard Gamone left money to the lights. He gave money for Our Lady Light, which was next to an image of the Virgin Mary, as well the 'hokkyng light'. There was also the Trinity Light, St Katherine's Light, Holy Cross, Plow Light and the Sepulchre Light. The Trinity was near to the rood screen, separating the chancel from the nave, while the 'hokkyng light' flickered on Hoke Day after Easter and the Sepulchure Light burned during Holy Week.

The super wealthy left money for a chantry so that when they died a priest sang a mass for their soul to speed its journey through purgatory to heaven. In 1335, Henry de Bydyk left money in his will for a chantry for one year in St Mary the Virgin and in 1442 Sir William Tirwhit founded a chantry in a chapel, which stood in a field next to Higham manor house on the lane to Chingford. It would give rise to the name of the settlement around it, Chapel End.

The priest was a great figure of authority in people's lives and the parishioners put up memorials in the church to honour the most influential. Sir Henry Crane was honoured with a brass memorial inscription after he died in 1437 and so was one of his successors, William Hyll, who died in 1485. The brass plate depicted Hyll in his ministering garments and with a tonsure, a shaved crown of hair on his head (as many medieval clerics had), and with his hands clasped in prayer.

The inscription on the memorial for Henry Crane in the parish church. (© Victoria and Albert Museum, London)

A settlement that became known as Church End clustered around the church. The property left in the will of Hyll suggests that Church End was a sizable place by the fifteenth century. There was the vicarage and a 'lytall place' the vicar owned at the church gate and another house he left to Elizabeth Bircher, as well a house with an orchard standing before the cottage of the sexton, John Hews. Hyll also left a tiled house with a croft, which was an enclosed area of land, standing near to the vicarage. An inn owned by John Maughtel stood on the highway leading to the church.

The highway was one of a number of streets and lanes in the medieval parish. The principal street was Mershstrete, or Marsh Street, or the way to the meadows, which led from the marshland up towards the church on the hill. It was so well used that William Cockerell left 20*s* in his will for its repair in 1434. Other important streets were Hoe Strete, Claystrete and Wodestrete, or Wood Street. Shornwellstrete took its name from the Old English words *scearn*, meaning 'dung, filth', and *wielle* for spring, as it led down to the Fillebrook stream, which had become polluted by animal and human waste. As dwellings clustered along these streets, people started to live in street-villages on these main roads. At Higham Hill there were ten or so dwellings grouped in a hamlet on the lane to Chapel End and each building stood on its own tenement of land with a *hoppet* (a small meadow) and crofts nearby.

The lanes linked the medieval manors to a wider world. There was Amberland Lane to Chingford and lanes led to the abbeys at Waltham Holy Cross, Barking and Stratford Langthorne, which had markets by 1225. Visitors arrived by the lanes. On 10 February 1208, King John and his retinue of servants stayed for two nights in Walthamstow before travelling on. In 1220 a thief named William Smallwood, who had been on a robbery and murder spree, appeared in Walthamstow after arriving from another part of Essex. He had two horses stolen from a nobleman and hid at the inn of Hugh Large, who ended up on trial in front of the Justices of the Bench. The innkeeper was paid 6*s* for keeping the horses hidden away for eight days

St Mary's Church after the medieval church was rebuilt and extended. (Courtesy of London Metropolitan Archives)

while a woman who worked there received 6*d* for bringing them water so they were out of sight.

The route to London crossed the marshes, which were difficult to cross in the winter because of flooding. But people were aware of events in the city. In 1377, during the Peasants' Revolt, Paul de Salesbury, whose family owned Salisbury Hall, settled scores with William Baret, an alderman, by turning up at his London house with a mob of men, including his servant Thomas, who were armed with swords and staffs and demanding the title of the property be transferred to him. He then ransacked the house of Hugh Falstof at St Dunstan, insisting tenements be leased to him and threatening to behead Hugh. They stole a sword and drank six casks of ale during the rampage. De Salesbury was indicted as one of the rebels in 1381 but was pardoned by the king.

The maintenance of the lanes was the responsibility of the manors. Rectory Manor, made up of lands given by Alice in 1108, remained the property of Holy Trinity Priory but other manors experienced dizzying changes of ownership. Walthamstow Toni remained in the de Toni family until 1309, but part was broken off to form the smaller Walthamstow Bedyk or Low Hall

Manor. The larger manor passed by marriage to the Beauchamp family, the earls of Warwick and then to other owners. After Domesday Book, Higham passed from Peter de Valognes by marriage to Alexander de Baliol, and was bought in 1323 by John de Bensted. At some point it was subdivided as well. A slice around the River Ching was bought by Sir William Tirwhit and called Salisbury Hall, who held it under Margaret Plantagenet, the Countess of Salisbury. These manors also had the seat of the owner, many of whom may have been at the Walthamstow manor infrequently, who often lavished money on buildings. In the fourteenth century a new manor house was built near to today's Low Hall Lane for Low Hall Manor. It had a moat – which were common in rural areas and increasingly a status symbol rather than for defence – kitchen, garderobe, hall with a fireplace, bakery and upstairs living quarters offering privacy. A manor house at Salisbury Hall was built near to a crossing at the Ching, and Walthamstow Toni's house was built as High Hall on Clay Street.

Manors regulated the affairs of the estate through the manorial courts and the officials who helped to run the demesne farm and collect rents. The Court Leet, which managed civil matters such as appointing ale-conners to regulate ale brewing and constables. The Court Baron oversaw land transfers and dealt with disputes between tenants. Most land was copyhold, which meant a fee was paid each year and the name of a tenant was written onto the manorial roll. These tenants, even in the fourteenth century, still had labour obligations as their *villein* and *bordar* ancestors had done. In 1369 John Millere, who rented a cottage and 8 acres of land in the Langhege or Long Hedge field from Rectory Manor, had to scour ditches as his customary work for the manor.

The manor officials wrote detailed records. There is a *computus* or accounting statement of rents for Walthamstow Toni, compiled by the collector Andrew Swete from 1437–8, which shows how he worked alongside John Smyth (the reeve) and John Yonge (the bailiff) to manage the manor and collect rents for land. Rents may have fallen because there was less demand after epidemics like the Black Death (which, according to local legend, led to corpses being emptied into plague pits in the churchyard) reduced the population. The 1377 Walthamstow poll tax returns show that only 242 people were eligible to pay the tax.

Walthamstow Toni's land was considerable, including large fields such as the 12-acre Horscrofte and 18-acre Stonydowne. Callewellelond was 22 acres and Stannecotehogge, where there must have been a pig house, was 27 acres and brought in £4 13*s* 4*d* a year. Since 1433 John Yonge had leased a farm of 62 acres at Eggepulmershe for 26*s* 8*d*. He also had 4 acres in the Uplond and a piece of land called Grenedormes containing 10 acres.

As well as farming, the bailiffs also rounded up stray animals. They collected rents from smaller tenants. Margaret Stephenes made a living from husbandry and market gardening. She leased an apple orchard for 5*s*; paying 3*s* 4*d* a year to lease pasture called Le Broke and Le Connynger, a field name suggesting a former rabbit warren. Her main farming was on pasture called Fysshepond. Robert Marcheford leased the 10-acre South Litulmersshe for 6*s*, and paid 14*s* a year to rent the Beweicheshote, a 30-acre site. The farm of Grenepond, where a brook fed the ponds, was leased for 40*s* a year to William Lane, who also rented Tassherescrofte.

The watermill had always been a highly profitable asset for the manor. John Asshud was the miller in 1437–38 and paid a mill rent of 23*s* 4*d* a year. He was also renting the land on which the mill stood, called Le Millholme, for 13*s* 4*d*, which was almost certainly where the site of the Domesday mill stood. Asshud was also leasing Oxelesewe by the River Lea as pasture to graze cattle for 20*s*.

The manors managed land which was the property of minors as well. Since 1405 John Webbe of Claystrete or Clay Street had farmed 10 acres of Lytulnorthmershe, paying 6*s* 8*d* a year. In 1427, after Richard Webbe died, it was left to his 3-year-old daughter Matilda in wardship, meaning it was held by the manor until she came of age. Until then, the manor pocketed 2*s* 8*d* a year.

The manorial records also documented important social changes. The Normans brought new names, which obviously became popular among the ordinary folk who stopped using the Old English personal names and switched to names such as Matilda and Robert, which the Normans had called their children. The records also show that ordinary people adopted a hereditary surname and not just a byname, which had often just been their occupation or nickname.

Since Domesday the amount of land farmed and cultivated had increased because of the 'assarting' into the forest to clear woodland. At Higham a chunk of Sayle Wood was enclosed after 1284, the trees felled and the land broken up for tillage. At Sale wood and in other places this land was called Le Braches, from an Old English word for 'breaking' to signify that there was new ground. The 'woodland for 300 pigs' recorded in the Domesday Book was cleared steadily. The clearance led to new settlements. In 1285 the place name Hale, from the Old English *halh*, meaning a nook in a river bend, was recorded for the settlement near the Ching. It later became known as Hale End.

Peasants colonised marshland near the River Lea to create meadows. Over generations they built earth banks along the edges of the marshland and cut ditches into the terrain to drain off the water to leave small parcels of meadow. This back-breaking work gradually developed the enormous open meadow running down to the River Lea called the common marsh, where the vicar William Hyll had an acre which he donated to the churchwardens in his will, as well as large enclosed meadows such as Cockerell's marsh. All were prized for their hay crop.

Hyll also left acres of arable land in the Buryfield, one of Walthamstow's three open fields. These were enormous unenclosed fields of mainly arable land. The Buryfield at Church End was the smallest of the three fields while the largest was the Mill Field at Higham Hill, followed by the Bromefield off Mark Lane leading to Leyton. Inside the open fields to which the land cultivated by the twenty-two men's ploughs recorded in Domesday Book may have been a reference, there was no enclosure by hedges so the small strips of land scattered around were marked out with small stones known as *metes* and *dooles*.

While most worked their own land in the meadows or arable fields, the larger peasant farmers hired labourers. Some of these workers were even born far outside the parish. Records of taxes called 'alien subsidies', a tax levied on immigrants, show that there were people born outside England. In 1444, a migrant labourer named Dedericus Lambe, possibly a Fleming, was working in Walthamstow, while the yeoman John Pender had a foreign servant named Janyn.

The *computus* shows that rent had to be paid. Some people has always got into debt. In 1369, Robert Mannyng owed £22 5*s* to Nicholas Ploket of London, and was being chased by his creditor. Simon Wynde, who bought the meadow from the priory, had by the 1370s built up landholdings and had a farmstead with 28 acres of arable land and 2 acres of meadow. But he was struggling to pay his enormous debt of £21 4*s* 8*d*. His creditors seized his seven geese, fourteen ducks, twenty bushels of oats hay, straw and vetch, and his lead trough and grindstone.

Walthamstow's land market, often driven by wealthy outsiders, experienced boom and bust. In 1347 William Martyn, a parson of East Peckham, bought a *messuage*, a farmstead with outbuildings, 80 acres of land and 9 acres of meadow for 100 marks. But by 1414 Richard Clerk, a citizen of London, bought a *messuage* with the same amount of land and 16 acres of meadow for just 20 marks. Land buying as an investment continued until the end of the medieval period. But there were some wealthy outsiders who bought estates for farming in Walthamstow and settled down to stay. One of them was the wealthy Londoner George Monoux, who acquired a farmstead in the sixteenth century and would have a profound effect on the parish.

4

Almshouses, Alehouses and Religion in a Tudor Town

Walthamstow underwent rapid change in the sixteenth century as new wealth led to the rebuilding of the parish church, the construction of large dwellings and the foundation of almshouses, while traditional religious worship was overturned, leading to some people to become set apart from the majority in the parish.

The new wealth was brought into Walthamstow by a rising commercial class represented by George Monoux, an extremely wealthy master of the Worshipful Company of Drapers and a former Lord Mayor of London, who bought a farm called De Moones on the lane to Chapel End in the early sixteenth century. Monoux had retired from trade and commerce for good and for the next decades of his life settled down to dedicate himself to good works for the parish.

George Monoux and others started by rebuilding the parish church. In 1535 a new brick tower was built with Monoux's money, along with a chapel and a north aisle. He even paid for the bells to be rung morning and night twice a year. Walthamstow also had other benefactors. Robert Thorn, a merchant taylor of London whose ancestors were connected with the church, helped to rebuild the south aisle in 1535, and William Lee donated money to repair the roof. They ensured that their donations were known about. In a window of the church was installed the Monoux coat of arms in stained glass. On another window of the church, which was later removed, the worshippers would have looked up to read the transcription: 'Christen people praye for the soule of Robert Thorn, citizen of London, with whose goodys thys syde of thys church was newe edyfyd and fynyshed'.

Monoux's good works extended to education. In 1541 he left an endowment in his will for a chantry, or *obit* as it was also called, which was to be sung once a year by an alms-priest for the soul of Monoux and his late wife Ann in the new chapel. It was to be paid for from rents on property he owned in Fenchurch Street, and Mark Lane in London. But the alms-priest had another role as a schoolteacher and he was to be assisted by a parish clerk in the church and to help teach 30 or so children of the parish at a school, which would be free to attend.

The good works were a demonstration of faith as well as a display of wealth. When Monoux died in 1543 he was entombed with his wife Ann, who had died before him, in the new chapel. Fixed on the wall above the tomb were Monoux's coat of arms and brass figures of the husband and wife kneeling in prayer. There is an inscription next to Ann with the words: 'O Lord, give unto us thy salvation.' The brasses are today on a pillar at St Mary's.

The schoolmaster, who retained the title of alms-priest, must have been a widely respected figure. One of the first schoolteachers was a 40-year-old former clerk named John Hogeson, who in 1547 was described as of 'good vsage and conversacion, literate'. Many of the schoolmasters felt a bond with the parish in which they taught and in 1609 Thomas Colby, the serving alms-priest and schoolmaster who died of the plague, left all his goods and money to the poor. The schoolmaster and clerk appear to have been able to teach their own curriculum. In later centuries Monoux's chapel became a grammar school teaching Latin and Greek but there is nothing to suggest that

The brass of George Monoux in St Mary's Church.

the first pupils studied anything other than reading, writing and arithmetic. However, there were people living in the sixteenth-century parish with a classical education, such as George Gascoigne, the Elizabethan dramatist, who died in Walthamstow. Nonetheless, by offering free schooling, Monoux's chapel was a revolution in education for the parish.

Good works also helped the poor. The children at Monoux's school were taught in a schoolroom above almshouses built by Monoux on land just north of the churchyard. By the 1540s or thereabouts the brick almshouses had been built for thirteen almsfolk: eight men and five women. The almshouses, which still stand today, were on two storeys with six rooms on the west wing and seven on the east of the ground floor. Each room had a fireplace, two windows and two doors. In the centre on the upper floor were the alms-priest's and schoolmaster's rooms and on one side a gallery room in which he taught.

Almsfolk lived under strict rules. To be admitted they had to kneel before the crucifix at St Mary's, say the Lord's Prayer and a Hail Mary five times, and attend Mass daily. Visiting the alehouse was banned, as was going away overnight or allowing visitors to stay in their rooms. They were cared for,

A view of George Monoux's almshouses built in the sixteenth century. (Courtesy of London Metropolitan Archives)

Inside the schoolroom at the Monoux almshouses, pictured in the nineteenth century. (Courtesy of Vestry House Museum, London Borough of Waltham Forest)

however, as Monoux ensured in the endowment that each of the almsfolk was paid 7*d* weekly and received coal in the winter to burn in the fireplace in their room. They had a patch of land at the back of the almshouses for use as a garden, in which they hung out their clothes to dry in the sun.

Walthamstow's poor were also helped by smaller gifts. At the church there was a poor box, and Robert Fynchley left 12*d* to the poor in his will and a shirt to Nicholas Gekon, who lived in the almshouses. In 1599 Elizabeth Alford left money for the almsfolk, to be paid on the feast of St Bartholomew and St Thomas, and every Ash Wednesday they were given herrings.

Good works were also directed to improving the roads and infrastructure. In 1547 Paul Withipol left 20*l.* to mend the roads, and Monoux paid for a wooden causeway to be built over Walthamstow marshes leading to the Lock Bridge over the Lea. The bridge was an important crossing point for market folk travelling by foot to the markets in London from Walthamstow and other parishes and meant the marshes could be crossed in winter. And the parish was growing. By the 1540s Walthamstow was recorded as 'a greate town' and was estimated to have '18 score howselynge people and more' who attended Holy Communion at the church, so perhaps there were about 700 or so inhabitants.

A sign of this development is the Ancient House, as it became known, which still stands today on the corner of Orford Road and Church Lane, opposite the parish church. Dendrochronology has shown that it was built in the late sixteenth century, although some of the timber used could be from the fourteenth century. At first the Ancient House was a square-shaped hall house built with a wooden frame and walls made of interwoven wattle and willow wands covered in plaster and a lime-wash daub. The dwelling was originally just one room open to the rafters with no ceiling, so that smoke rose up from the fire and escaped from a louvre of wooden slats in the roof. But in later years cross-halls were added to either end of the hall and a first floor was installed with dormer glass windows, which were no doubt quite an expense at the time. Another improvement was installing two stone fireplaces and a brick chimney to expel the fug of smoke and clear the air inside. The first inhabitants were superstitious, placing two charms in the timbers to ward off ill fortune.

The town had plenty of alehouses. They were increasingly viewed with suspicion as harbouring vagrants and beggars and encouraging games of cards or dice in a period when nearly all games apart from archery were banned. Thomas Gates, the parish clerk, was caught playing unlawful games of dice and cards. Alehouses had to be licensed by the county court sessions and magistrates were on the lookout for unlicensed establishments. A typical alehouse had tables and benches and drinkers supped from pint or quart earthenware and stone pots or larger vessels for communal drinking.

Alehouses and brewing ale was an important area of work for women. In 1504, Agnes Moreys and Agnes Munden were fined 2*d* by the Court

Detail of the wood-framed Ancient House built in the sixteenth century opposite the parish church. Note the old dormer glass windows. (Courtesy of Vestry House Museum, London Borough of Waltham Forest)

Leet at Salisbury Hall for selling their ale by goblets rather than in the correct measure after being caught by the ale-conner. In 1580, Alice Hamonde was granted a licence and in 1590 the widow Syslye Graves was licensed to run an alehouse.

Husbandmen and yeomen also ran alehouses as a sideline and profits were reinvested in land, which some families were accumulating rapidly. In 1589 George Monoux's son sold Moons Farm to a yeoman named Thomas Hale. Moons had a substantial amount of arable and pasture as well as a grove, woodyard, orchard and a hop garden, and the brick farmhouse was surrounded by a moat. The Hale family added to the farm by building a bakehouse and dairy on part of the orchard. Increasing wealth meant that these yeomen families lived in greater domestic comfort in their farms. In 1559 William Mannyng, perhaps a descendant of the medieval bankrupt Robert, and his wife Catheryne slept in a bedroom chamber with 'hangyngs' of linen covering the walls and at mealtime had a saltcellar, candlesticks, pewter platters and saucers for serving food placed on their table.

Large landowners such as Ralph Sadler, a privy counsellor to Henry VIII, and owner of Low Hall Manor, were doing well in the sixteenth century. Sadler's manorial officials reported to him the considerable amounts his lands were making. In 1559 two butchers from St Nicholas Shambles in London named Mr Bramley and Mr Peperd were renting the pasture known as the Butchers Marsh, approximately 70 acres. A goodman (a small farmer) from the Sygne of the Swan on Mylkestrete was also a tenant farmer. Sadler had acres in the common marsh that he leased as well as two 'lytell' closes 'letten to tow pooremen of Wolthamstow for one yere'. There was also Busshe Marshe, which had 'herable land', arable land for growing crops, and a 'howse, and barne and stable' rented to a tenant named Sparowe.

The valuable meadows, which were on the low-lying land near to the Lea, were a constant battle to keep dry. The tenants of Low Hall had to 'skore the greate dyches that goeth alonge in the lane, frome the howse to the ryver' so that the water drained off, and scour ditches near to Butchers Marshe. But it was a struggle to maintain the meadows as good pasture and the official found that Bushe Marsh was 'clene over growen with thornes'.

While landowners and yeomen prospered, the labouring poor were falling further behind in their share of this new wealth. Labourer George Furnifall's will left just a mare and clothing to his son Nathaniel, two shillings to his daughter Agnes and whatever was left of his meagre possessions to his wife Alice. That was despite wages being regulated under the Statute of Artificers by the court sessions, which in 1574 stipulated that the yeoman John Golding should pay Richard Hankyn, John Nevell and Agnes Well a 20-shilling rate. But wealth was not the only division in the sixteenth-century parish.

In 1532 the vicar Thomas Hyckman, who had been appointed by the Holy Trinity Priory, led the traditional services at St Mary the Virgin. A rood screen with the figure of Christ and saints' statues separated the priest in the chancel from the laity while Hyckman read from an illuminated service book and said prayers in Latin. However, King Henry VIII was introducing new religious policies and that year the Holy Trinity Priory was one of the religious institutions suppressed. Through Rectory Manor the Priory had been an important landholder with tenants such as John Sawer who, just before suppression, were allowed to rent the 2-acre Brooks Croft near Prioures Street by Master Hancok, the Prior. But when Hyckman retired in 1534 the prior was gone and the king's commissioners appointed a new vicar. The manor's land was sold off.

That wasn't the only change. The alms-priest appointed by the Monoux endowment would have sung few Masses because, by 1547, chantry chapels had been outlawed as well. The *obits* at the parish church and the chapel near to Higham manor house were stopped. In 1549 a new prayer book was introduced into the parishes and services were said in English rather than Latin. By 1559 everyone in the parish aged 18 and over had to attend St Mary the Virgin on a Sunday and the seven lights for which Richard Gamone and other generations had left money were removed, apart from two candles lit at the altar.

There were those who welcomed the reformed faith. Many of them would have read, or heard recited aloud *The Acts and Monuments*, John Foxe's account of Protestant martyrdom and lessons for living a godly life, which was a popular printed book in the sixteenth century. According to Foxe, in 1563 William Mauldon and his wife had moved to Walthamstow where his wife taught children to read. Mauldon's wife overheard a 12-year-old girl named Denis Benfielde blaspheme and call God an 'olde doting foole'. After Mauldon heard 'these abhominable woordes of the girle', he urged his wife to speak to Benfielde's daughter. But it was too late. The next day while returning from a market in London, the girl was struck down and died. Foxe's message was stark: even children were expected to be godly.

The vicar was still an important figure of authority to his flock for religious guidance. Even in the late sixteenth century, during the years of religious turmoil, the vicar George Johnson was committed to leading the parishioners at St Mary's and did so for a decade. When he died in 1576, a plaque with an image of him speaking in the pulpit was put up. The first four lines read:

> The Office set by Pastor true,
> By Christ his Flock to guide,
> Is unto them his Faith to preach,
> And from it never slide.

But not everyone was attending the parish church to hear Johnson or the other vicars. Walthamstow had families of Roman Catholics who remained loyal to the old faith. The Hale family, who now rented Moones Farm in which there was a private chapel built by Monoux, were prominent recusants or non-attenders at church and Thomas Hale the elder and his wife Ann were prosecuted for twenty years or so. In 1582 the magistrates noted that Thomas Hale had refused to attend Holy Communion 'for consyence sake'.

Members of the Hale family were frequently fined at the Quarter Sessions as recusants. In 1588 one of Hale's sons, also called Thomas, was imprisoned. He was forced to write to the Archbishop of Canterbury, 'declaringe his duetifull alleageaunce unto her Majestie' and confessing his 'longe sickenes'. Thomas's brothers Richard and Austin, and their sisters Elizabeth, Katherine and Jane, were also fined. In 1593 a man named Edward Godfre discovered at Moones verses in the hand of the young Thomas Hale. Hale was held in the new Bridewell House of Correction in London until he stood trial at the assizes in 1594 for libel, at which the full text and Hale's supposed authorship was examined by the magistrates. The text followed the melody of 'Weepe, Weepe', a popular ballad, and expressed dismay at the persecution of the old faith. Hale pleaded not guilty to seditious libel, claiming he merely copied out the text and it seems that the first stanza was lifted from a broadside by the sixteenth-century balladeer William Elderton. He was set free.

The deeply religious George Monoux had been an exception when he retired to Walthamstow from London. But by the seventeenth century the parish was becoming hugely popular with merchants and other members of the capital's commercial classes, who were growing in number and began flocking to the parish and building on a scale that Monoux could not have imagined.

5

Merchants, Mansions and Poachers: A Seventeenth-Century Parish

In the seventeenth century Walthamstow experienced a wave of development as merchants and London's commercial classes spent their considerable wealth on rebuilding properties and erecting mansions which dwarfed the cottages of just one or two hearths in which the majority of people lived.

Walthamstow was enormously attractive to London's wealthy because it only lay around 8 miles from the New Royal Exchange and the City of London and was, by the seventeenth century, in reach of the express postal service. The scenic Essex parish, which had a large covering of forest, was the perfect place in which to relax and recover from a hectic commercial life or affairs of state and had plenty of old dwellings which could be snapped up as a country house.

One of the first of these rising families was the Conyers. The family originated in North Yorkshire and had made money in shipping but two of the younger members, Tristram and Robert, established themselves in London. Robert was a successful merchant and by the early seventeenth century Tristram had acquired Low Hall Manor and other property in Walthamstow, including most of the land around Hoe Street, . His nephew, William, inherited the land. To remember his uncle, in 1621 William set up a benefaction overseen by the churchwardens which gave out twelve three-penny loaves of bread to the poor every Sunday, placing the bread on Monoux's tomb during the divine service.

Other members of the new wealthy rose through the City's livery companies. Edward Corby had been born into a poor family in Walthamstow in 1613 and was put out as an apprentice by the parish into the Cook's Company and became a freeman, making a fortune and buying land in the parish. When Corby died in 1674 he left tenements in Wood Street to the churchwardens, stipulating that 3*l*. 15*s* from the rents and profits be given to the poor every year.

Merchants settled in Walthamstow who had made a fortune in overseas trade. William Coward, who arrived in the 1670s to buy copyhold land and build a house on Marsh Street, had owned a plantation in Jamaica and a fleet of ships sailing on the trade routes from the Port of London to the West Indies, one of which was called the *Walthamstow Galley*. He was a religious dissenter who supported nonconformist congregations. A dissenting community had been established in Walthamstow and the preacher, Samuel Slater, was licensed in 1672 under the Act of Toleration as a Presbyterian teacher and his home on Marsh Street was licensed as a meeting house. Coward, who, according to a map of Walthamstow Toni by Alexander Forbes drawn in 1699, owned a lot of land along Marsh Street, supported the community. Their religious brethren visited them from the capital to preach and Coward gave enough land in Marsh Street for a permanent meeting house to be built in 1695.

Most merchants worshipped at the parish church. They married at St Mary's, cementing alliances with London's wealthy. The civil register of marriages, introduced in 1652, shows a growing number of local women were marrying men from London. Dorothy Conyers married a London gentleman named Stephen Harvey in 1654, and Alice Collard wed Thomas Woodman of the Parish of St Albans in 1655. Some members of the local gentry married into the capital's commercial classes, including Charles Maynard, who, in the 1630s, was the Lord of Walthamstow Toni and married Mary, a daughter of the London merchant Zeger Corfellis, founding a family of merchants. One of their grandsons, Henry, was even a leading merchant in the Ottoman Empire.

The parish church had seen increasing disturbances regarding religious matters. In 1649 a haberdasher named William Harding was summoned to the Essex Quarter Sessions 'to answer for certain misdemeanours' committed in the parish church. Harding's crime was almost certainly to do with the new vicar, John Wood, who had been put in place by the Committee for Plundered Ministers, set up by Parliament to silence clergy who remained loyal to the King. He proved extremely unpopular with many of the parishioners. Commissioners investigating church appointments for Parliament noted that 'he is now questioned for his abilities' and that he was so disliked that most people refused to attend church, 'whereby there is great distraction in the parish'.

Discord about church policy and religious matters helped to push the nation into civil war. Walthamstow's new residents sided with Parliament, as did many people in the parish such as a yeoman farmer who supplied Parliament's armies with food and was imprisoned by Royalists for doing so. But there were members of the gentry who favoured the king. Landowner Thomas Merry, who lived with his wife Mary at Winns House in Clay Street, had a sinecure as the Clerk Comptroller of the Green Cloth and was a Royalist. After the war his lands were seized, although the family's alabaster monument with busts of Sir Thomas and Mary Merry was erected in St Mary's Church.

Monument of the Merry family in St Mary's Church.

The commercial classes welcomed the development of industry in the parish. During the English Civil War, the watermill was converted to make gunpowder by John Samyne, who leased the site from Walthamstow Toni manor. At the height of Samyne's production there were three powder mills, two in Clerk's Holme and one in Smithy Marsh, making four barrels a day. The mills later produced leather and by the 1690s they were converted to paper manufacture, making high-quality white writing paper for the capital's luxury market.

Brickmaking was a growing cottage industry as people rebuilt old Tudor houses in brick or constructed new buildings. Farmhouses such as Moons Farm was rebuilt with a new barn in the seventeenth century. A map of Walthamstow Toni by Alexander Forbes in 1699 shows a brick kiln field owned by Coward off Marsh Street and another to the north of Clay Street owned by Thomas Wilson, and a Tile Kiln Hill near to Woodford. The wave of building started with the Conyers, who rebuilt an old Tudor house on the south side of Hoe Street, just opposite where Grosvenor Park Road is today, and which guidebooks would call 'a fair and graceful house in Hoo Street'. The 1670 returns for the Hearth Tax – a property tax on the number of hearths or fireplaces – shows the extent of building in seventeenth-century Walthamstow. It listed a mansion owned by Sir William Holcroft with seventeen hearths, while William Maynard boasted sixteen and the Conyers' property had fifteen hearths.

The commercial classes often owned houses in London as well as a rural retreat in Walthamstow. Daniel Defoe later commented that the building wave in the rural parishes around the capital was 'chiefly for the habitations of the richest citizens, such as either are able to keep two houses, one in the country, and one in the city.' These second home owners included Elizabeth Bernard, a member of a wealthy family which lived in Walthamstow, who in 1683 left a property in her will at Durham Yard near the New Royal Exchange. The boom was strongest from the end of the seventeenth century. At Walthamstow, Low Leyton, Stratford and other places in the lower Lea Valley, 'above a thousand new foundations have been erected, besides old houses repaired, all since the [Glorious] Revolution,' noted Defoe, 'and this is not to be forgotten too, that this increase is, generally speaking, of handsom [*sic*] large houses'. The area's property values and rents boomed as new money poured in.

Elizabeth Batten, who owned three houses in 1670, was a typical newcomer. She had moved to Walthamstow in the 1660s with her late husband Sir William Batten, a surveyor of the Navy and friend of the diarist Samuel Pepys, who had other well-to-do friends in Walthamstow including

North end of the old barn at Moon's Farm, built around 1700 and demolished in 1927. (Courtesy of Vestry House Museum, London Borough of Waltham Forest)

Sir William Penn. At the Battens' property, which is thought to have been the old Rectory manor house, there was, according to Pepys, a fine study with a collection of good books.

Pepys enjoyed socialising at Walthamstow's grand houses. He would arrive to gossip with Mrs Browne or dine at the Battens' house and play billiards. A typical evening in 1661 was spent at Sir William Penn's home, where they had 'a good supper, and sat playing at cards and talking till 12 at night'. There would be good conversation and a mix of London guests, with country gentlemen and ladies at the table. Wine was the favoured tipple at dinner and at the Battens' house he drank a wine made with grapes grown on local vines. But Pepys also enjoyed the local beer. On 1 November 1660 the friends stumbled from William Batten's house and into the alehouse by the parish church, 'where we sat and drank and were merry' before riding back to London that night.

As well as entertaining, the houses were places for discussing business affairs. On 13 April 1662 Pepys, Sir William Penn and Batten talked over a petition to the king about the affairs of the Admiralty with a glass or two of wine. Pepys even sampled country life at Walthamstow, attending a service at the parish church on 5 July 1663, at which 'an old doting parson preached' and, to keep himself awake, he flicked through a book of Latin plays he had in his pocket.

For the incomers a stagecoach was essential for shuttling back and forth to London. Defore learned that there were 'no less than two hundred coaches kept by the inhabitants' in Walthamstow and the Lea Valley parishes. When Sir William Batten died there were said to be more than 100 stagecoaches in the procession travelling up to Walthamstow for the burial at the church. However, the Londoners antagonised the locals. On 18 April 1661, after a day of drinking, Pepys and Penn met two country fellows on horseback going the other way. Pepys gave way, but Sir William refused. Pepys recorded:

> Sir W. Pen would not, but struck them and they him, and so passed away, but they giving him some high words, he went back again and struck them off their horse, in a simple fury, and without much honour, in my mind.

The extra traffic of stagecoaches may have helped to damage the roads, which the parish struggled to maintain in the seventeenth century. Mill Lane, leading to Tottenham, which King James I had travelled, was particularly bad and deemed a hazard for anyone to ride on but especially 'for a stranger that knowe it not'. The parish's surveyors of the highways weren't helped by a reluctance of labourers to do the days' work allocated to them or a refusal by some gentlemen to make their carts available for hauling gravel or sand.

The mansions also had servants including maids, house servants and coachmen. Pepys, who had been a Roundhead as a boy, disliked the crudeness with which Mrs Batten or Sir William Penn spoke to or treated their servants. On 13 September 1667 he was annoyed to hear Penn's tantrum at his coachman after arriving in Walthamstow and finding his wife was still in London. He wrote:

> bidding his coachman in much anger to go for them (he being vexed, like a rogue, to do anything to please his wife), his coachman Tom was heard to say a pox, or God rot her, can she walk hither?

Venison was a favourite meal of Pepys and he loved a dinner of venison or snacking on a hot venison pasty at the Battens' house in Walthamstow. Deer were abundant in the Forest of Waltham and woodland still covered a sizable chunk of the parish. But it was extremely expensive and a meat of the wealthy as hunting deer in the forest was a privilege still reserved for the Crown. The forest was divided into ten 'Walks', enclosed and fenced-off areas of woodland reserved for royal hunting, which were patrolled by foresters and keepers. The only way the labouring poor could eat venison was by poaching deer.

Walthamstow was then surrounded by Waltham Forest, known at other times as the Forest of Essex. As well as the Walks, there were courts managed by officials called verderers, and a forest law. The Stuart kings used this legal system to extract fines and raised revenues from those living inside the forest by penalising them for any encroachment. In the 1630s Tristam Conyers was fined for building a dwelling years before, as was John Browne, who had built a cottage.

Poaching was rampant as gangs of men with dogs laid nets and traps and shot at the valuable deer with muskets, crossbows, and bows and arrows. In 1642, a blacksmith from Walthamstow named Thomas Page and a gang of five men attacked a forester who had disturbed them while they trapped a doe and a stag worth 10*s* each. A mob of fifteen or so men from Chingford stalked around Walthamstow Walk at night and killed a red deer worth 10*s*. In 1643 Clement Godfery, a weaver, farmer Richard Cooper and George Scott, a labourer, killed a buck they caught in Rydden Grove in Walthamstow worth 20*s*.

Stealing deer was nothing new. Poaching had existed since the forest laws were introduced by the Anglo-Saxon kings, but in the seventeenth century deer stealers were rampant. Sir William Holcroft, a verderer of the forest, received printed notices giving the names of the most active poachers in the forest.

Many of the poachers had scant regard for authority. In 1652, Thomas Page was accused at the Quarter Sessions of speaking 'certen scandalous words' against the Commonwealth. The authorities were deeply concerned that the poachers operated in organised gangs, which had a spirit of fraternity and combination, and passed an Act in 1692 increasing fines for illegal hunting and being in possession of venison, and extended powers to search suspects' homes.

The renewed poaching took place amid greater hardship for many. The largest group of people recorded in the 1670 Hearth Tax for Walthamstow were poor cottagers whose homes were just one or two hearths. They included the widow Margeret Trunkett, who lived in a cottage with one hearth. When she died in 1675 all she left her sons Ralph and John was 12*s* each, while youngest son Thomas got 2 acres of meadow, bed linen and a feather pillow. For the poorest, the forest was an important resource for timber and fuel and all ratepayers had the right to turn out cattle to pasture in the common areas.

Amid the building boom of merchants' houses, developing industry and commercial wealth, the number of poor people in the parish by the eighteenth century was rising as more people drifted in from London. The vestry now also had to deal with the 1662 Settlement Act, which gave anyone who had lived in a parish for forty days the right to a stay and claim poor relief. The vestry would now try an experiment to solve the problem, which few parishes had tried.

6

Chartists, Paupers and Apprentices: Walthamstow and the Industrial Revolution

In 1730 the stonemason Samuel Chandler carved an inscription inspired by the Bible on a headstone, which was placed over the doorway of the parish workhouse in Walthamstow: 'If any should not work, neither should he eat.'

The workhouse, built on a few acres of the Berry Field, was opened as a result of the vestry's alarm at the number of people applying for parish relief. It had started a temporary workhouse at Hoe Street in 1726, using a building rented from the stagecoach master Joseph Schooling, which had successfully reduced expenditure on poor relief by providing employment. Walthamstow was a wealthy parish, the vestry earned a large amount of income from a significant land portfolio, but wealthy ratepayers were determined that the poor rate, levied on their grand houses, should be kept down.

The able-bodied could still request relief outside the workhouse. In 1742 Robert Cooper was given 4*s* a week to support his wife and five children after a cart had run over his foot and he was unable to work. But there was a hardening of attitudes and the Overseers of the Poor ordered that badges with the letters WP (Walthamstow Parish) were to be sewn on to the right sleeve of a garment belonging to parishioners, who were receiving relief.

The parish workhouse building, pictured around 1900. The lock-up or 'cage' is the tiled building on the right. (Courtesy of Vestry House Museum, London Borough of Waltham Forest)

Workhouse paupers were mainly the elderly, children without parents, and the sick. The four boys of Jonathan Danday, who had abandoned them, were admitted and in 1742 Elizabeth Field was accepted after she fell sick. By 1743 there were thirty-two people in the workhouse, the oldest was aged 82, and more than half were children. Children were put out as apprentices and usually 'sent abroad' to London tradesmen. Martha Needham was apprenticed aged 12 to a tailor in Goodman's Fields in the capital and 14-year-old Thomas Clifford to a wig maker.

The workhouse was austere. A pauper wore a numbered uniform of a petticoat, apron and shoes for women and girls, and stockings, waistcoats and a hat for the men and boys. Old men were given a greatcoat, and old women a cloak. Men and women slept in separate chambers upstairs while the governor had his own rooms downstairs. There was also a room for vestry meetings. The diet was monotonous but nourishing: milk pottage for breakfast, meat and vegetables for dinner and a supper of bread, cheese and butter on a typical day. The only books available were the Bible, prayer books and instruction books. Bad language was banned. On Sunday all the paupers filed out of the workhouse to walk to the nearby parish church.

Work was the main activity of the day. In the spring and summer months the paupers rose at 5.30 a.m. and spent an hour reading Psalms or the Gospels. They then worked from 8.30 a.m. to 12 noon and again in the afternoon until 6 p.m. Prayers were said in the evening. At 8 p.m. friends could visit before bed at 9 p.m. Men and boys cultivated the garden and picked oakum, which was sold to the navy to make ropes, and there was a spinning wheel for the women and girls to spin jersey, flax and hemp, who also knitted stockings. Paupers could also be 'farmed out' to work at hay time or at harvest for a set rate.

The number of workhouse paupers rose steadily over the decades. It was expanded in 1756 because of a growing population in the parish. Periods of acute economic distress produced even more desperate people requesting relief. By the summer of 1840 there were 106 paupers living in the workhouse, despite the numbers being kept down by refusing to admit people without certificates of settlement. As late as 1837 paupers were being forced to leave the parish, including Mary Chapman and her children who were removed to Paddington, the Overseer Mr Wigram ignoring appeals to allow the family to stay.

A new poor law in 1834 compelled Walthamstow to join forces with seven other small parishes to form the West Ham Poor Law Union, which was managed by a board of guardians and managed relief across a huge area. There was no need for the parish to operate a separate workhouse so in 1841 the remaining paupers were transferred from Walthamstow to a Union workhouse built in Leytonstone, which was a forbidding and grim place.

The poor had always received charity. The churchwardens doled out bread and coal on a Sunday, paid for by the many benefactions left over the centuries. But by the time the Union workhouse opened, the old attitudes to charity had changed. Some parishioners viewed the churchwardens' charities as a source of patronage and disliked their influence on the Monoux almshouses and the new almshouses built in 1795 near to the parish church by Mary Squires. In 1840 the vicar of Walthamstow, William Wilson, warned in his *Manual of Useful Information* against what he called 'indiscriminate and reckless' charity, which hindered encouraging 'honest industry, prudence and sobriety'. According to Wilson, instead of giving money for the poor to receive loaves at the church gate, the wealthier parishioners should donate to the Cheap Clothing Society, from which the poor could buy garments at a reduced rate.

The poor had always been expected to know their place. At the parish church the wealthiest and well-to-do members of the congregation paid pew rents to sit in the galleries or a box pew while the poorest sat in their own free seats. But by the nineteenth century the poor could expect a knock on the door from a home missionary, often a woman, offering advice about making clothes, cooking and domestic economy, or inviting them to a Bible class.

One of the consequences of increasing poverty in the eighteenth century was rising crime. Walthamstow's mansions attracted gangs of housebreakers from London and there were highwaymen on the roads. But policing was primitive, with old punishment stocks and a lock-up built at the side of the workhouse, known as 'the cage', in which miscreants were placed. A parish police force was only started in 1830 and until then Walthamstow relied on old watchmen, who sat in watch-boxes armed with blunderbusses, to provide security at night. Punishment was just as archaic. Those caught stealing wood in the forest could expect to be tied to a cart and whipped as it was driven along Wood Street, until it reached the area which later became known as Whipps Cross.

Many of the middling sorts who had relocated to the parish from London were extremely security-conscious. Joseph Jeffreys, who lived in Wood Street, ensured that all the doors of his house were fastened and bolted at night and a pair of pistols was hung up in the kitchen just in case housebreakers called. Jeffreys had a lot of valuable goods. He had retired to Walthamstow from the capital after making a fortune as a butcher and was wealthy enough to have sent his niece Elizabeth, who lived with him, away to school. In his will he left her £1,000, land, and his late wife's gold watch. But in 1751 Jeffreys himself became a victim of one of Walthamstow's most notorious crimes, which became a national sensation.

Jeffreys and his niece lived a comfortable life. She would take one of Mr Schooling's stagecoaches to Low Leyton or London and the retired butcher, who was well-liked by his neighbours on Wood Street, enjoyed his retirement, visiting his friend William Gallant, a barber in Walthamstow, or meeting acquaintances at the Royal Oak to take tea. At home he entertained until late with suppers of boiled beef. He also liked a drop of beer, spending evenings at the Bald Face Stag Inn at Buckhurst Hill and staggering home a little the worse for wear.

Jeffreys had two servants: John Swan, a general servant whose rooms were on the same floor as the niece and uncle, and the maid Sarah Arnold, who lived in the garret. Jeffreys summoned his staff from his room by pulling on a wire rigged up to bells in their quarters. Swan worked in the garden and on Jeffreys' land, putting a horse to grass, and attended to the substantial garden at the back as well as waiting on Jeffreys. In 1751 the retired butcher took on another man named Thomas Matthews, who helped Swan to get in the year's hay harvest with a horse and cart.

Swan, who was the son of a journeyman brick-maker in Cambridgeshire, was a good-looking young man and a relationship developed between him

Wood Street in Walthamstow, sketched in the eighteenth century. (Reproduced by courtesy of Essex Record Office)

and Jeffreys' young niece, Elizabeth. She socialised with him, drinking at the Duke's Head on Wood Street or at another inn called The Buck, or visiting the alehouse near Walthamstow church. The servants Swan and Matthews also caroused in Stratford and Whitechapel's alehouses and inns, sometimes getting violently drunk and spending the night in the local parish lock-up.

Jeffreys strongly disapproved of his niece's relationship with Swan. By the summer of 1751, Elizabeth was with child and she and Swan plotted with Matthews, who was offered money, to kill her uncle, allowing her to claim the inheritance. But on the day Matthews backed out of the plot so Elizabeth and Swan shot Jeffreys with his pistol and stabbed him with his old butcher's knife, which he had kept at the house to remind him of his old trade. They tried to pretend the attack was the work of thieves who had broken in, and threw some of Jeffreys' silver tankards, pewter and silver spoons into a pond on the other side of Wood Street to make it look like there had been a robbery.

The trial of John Swan and Elizabeth Jeffreys at the Assizes in Chelmsford captivated the public's attention in 1752. Pamphlets were printed describing

Jeffreys' grisly last moments as he panted for life with Swan and Elizabeth at his bedside and accounts of the murder with all the ghoulish details appeared in the London daily newspapers. Some of the pamphlets put Elizabeth's side of the story, and she maintained that her uncle had maltreated her years before.

Swan and Elizabeth maintained their innocence, but Matthews gave evidence against them and they were found guilty and sentenced to death. On the day of their execution a large crowd gathered in Wood Street, expecting the sentence to be carried out there. Some residents had rented out their houses for the occasion or built platforms for spectators to hire to get a better view, but after Swan and Elizabeth were brought from gaol in Chelmsford they were hanged near the 6-mile stone in Epping Forest rather than Wood Street. Relatives buried Elizabeth, but Swan's body was hung in chains and his body left to rot.

Joseph Jeffreys on his deathbed, surrounded by John Swan and niece Elizabeth. (Courtesy of London Metropolitan Archives)

Jeffreys, like many householders in what was still an agricultural parish, grazed a horse in the meadows. The largest in the eighteenth century were the open meadows, known as the common marsh, owned in thin strips marked out with boundary posts, including William Hyll's acre left to the churchwardens in 1485. The ratepayers also had a common grazing right on the meadows, known as lammas rights, which meant any ratepayer could graze his or her horse or cattle on the marsh. The meadows were opened for common grazing on 13 August, or Old Lammas Day, after the hay had been cut and carted off, and stayed open until Old Lady Day on 6 April the next year. Livestock, which had to be marked by the marsh reeve, were turned out to graze on the hay stubble.

A parishioner also had common grazing rights on the three commons or open fields, which represented 230 or so acres altogether in Jeffreys' time. There had, however, been a shift from largely ploughed arable fields to pasture. In Forbes' map of 1699 they were marked as the Mill Field, Broomfield and Berry Field, which were the names by which they had been known since the medieval period. But by the late eighteenth century they were called Higham Common, Markhouse Common and Church Common, after most of the strips were switched to pasture. Higham Common at Higham Hill was still the largest, followed by Markhouse Common on Markhouse Lane and Church Common at Church End.

The commons had been gradually reduced in size over the centuries as chunks were enclosed at the edges to create separate fields. Forbes' cartography shows Higham Common was far larger in the seventeenth century than it appears in later maps. But in the eighteenth century there was an attempt to enclose all of the commons. Anthony Todd, who was Secretary of the Post Office and lived at the Elms in Marsh Lane, campaigned at a vestry meeting in 1765 for Walthamstow to apply to Parliament to enclose the commons as many other parishes were doing at the time. The vestry disagreed. Perhaps even some of the larger owners of land in the commons recognised that enclosure would hurt the labouring poor and were mindful of the increasing poor rates.

The grazing rights on the commons were extremely valuable for the landless because, unlike the common marsh or the forest, there was no cost for grazing livestock. From Old Michaelmas Day on 11 October the commons were opened: Higham and Church Common opened together each year and alternated with Markhouse Common in successive years. Cattle, horses and even flocks of sheep could be herded through the gate of the commons and turned out to pasture.

Walthamstow's commons survived long into the nineteenth century after they had been enclosed in many other rural parishes in England. John Coe's map of the parish produced in 1822 shows they were still intact with their long thin strips of land. But there were attempts to enclose the commons at the vestry in 1808 and again in 1828, which was stopped by a public campaign and petition. However, the enclosure process had been made easier by the 1840s and Parliament appointed commissioners in 1846 after appeals by landowners who held the strips of land in the commons as freehold and copyhold. In 1848 a valuer published his plans which consolidated the strips of the large owners such as Samuel Bosanquet, the Lord of Low Hall Manor, into fields enclosed by hedges and fencing. Promises were made that large parts would be left as perpetual common and for spade husbandry but in the end farmers with common grazing rights were awarded small plots for pasture, and the overseers got a few acres as allotments for the poor. By 1850 the three old commons were no more.

Agriculture was an important source of wealth in the parish. Even some of the successful town dwellers who had moved to Walthamstow enjoyed playing the role of gentleman farmers. The carpenter and architect Joel Johnson, who designed the Small Pox Hospital in St Pancras, bought a farm in 1774 after stepping down from his business and retiring to Walthamstow. But Johnson found farming laborious and by 1781 he had let out the farm, but kept a little pasture. The merchant William Dilwyn also tried his hand at farming. His father-in-law Lewis Weston owned High Hall and William bought the neighbouring Fullager's Farm, merging the two estates and building Higham Lodge. The Quaker merchant managed to combine his demanding mercantile interests and humanitarian campaigning with farming and attended to cutting the hay crop or visiting nearby Chingford Hall to buy a cow and a three-wheel cart.

Walthamstow's agriculture was orientated to meeting demand from London. The capital needed a gargantuan amount of hay to feed the city's horses and dairy cows and Smithfield Market had special days on which just hay and straw were sold. Carts would leave Walthamstow loaded with hay for the market and return with dung, which was so valuable as manure it was sometimes stolen. London also needed more meat. This meant that more land in Walthamstow was switched to pasture. By 1794 it was thought that most of the land in the enclosed fields and on the commons was pasture for grazing animals. At Low Hall Farm, John Hanson was breeding stock scientifically to improve the animal's weight. He organised fat-stock classes and once produced a 52-stone pig, which appeared at a prize show at

Smithfield Market. The grazier Charles Burrell, who was a tenant of Low Hall after Hanson, bred a huge amount of livestock on the meadows and his droves left for Smithfield three times a day.

The large farms employed agricultural labourers many of whom were skilled workers and in demand during the periods of agricultural prosperity. In 1790 a labourer named Robert Martin had saved up enough to leave his wife Mary £400 of East India Company annuities in his will. But there was also low pay and insecurity. By the summer of 1846 a drift from the land had created such a scarcity of agricultural labourers in Walthamstow and other parishes near to London that constables from N and K Divisions of the Metropolitan Police, which operated in Walthamstow from 1840, worked on the haymaking in the meadowlands while off duty. Pitchers and rakers received 5*s* a day while the more highly skilled mowers could earn up to 7*s* a day. All got an allowance of beer.

Agricultural labourers could increasingly find work in manufacturing. By 1812 there were 3,777 people and 638 families living in the parish, according to the newly established census, but the balance between industry and agriculture had changed, with trade and manufacture employing 253 heads of household compared with 220 in agriculture, while the other families were employed in crafts.

Manufacturing was largely cottage industries such as brickmaking. New brickfields were started around upper Marsh Street and brick kilns operated in the forest at Whipps Cross, which were marked on John Roque's map of the area. Demand was substantial. In 1726 John Skingle and his son Henry had supplied 80,000 stock bricks, 800 paving bricks and 7,450 roof tiles for the building of the parish workhouse, and there were new mansions built such as Winns in Clay Street in 1744 and the Chestnuts in Hoe Street. But the expensive items were brought in from outside such as Suffolk white bricks, which were used to build Grosvenor House in Hoe Street.

Craftsmen were also employed in workshops, such as Francis Wragg's who took over Joseph Schooling's coach business in 1759. To meet the growing demand for transport to London, Wragg and successive members of his family who took over the business ran daily stagecoach services from the Nag's Head Inn at Church End, next door to his premises, to Bishopsgate. Goods and wares were also moved by carriers (trains of wagons pulled by a team of horses) and Walthamstow had three carrier companies by 1834.

Walthamstow's mills were increasing manufacturing on the old stream site. In 1778 John Towers started to make linseed oil until he sold the mill to George Shepley, who installed a 20ft-wide breast-water wheel, which

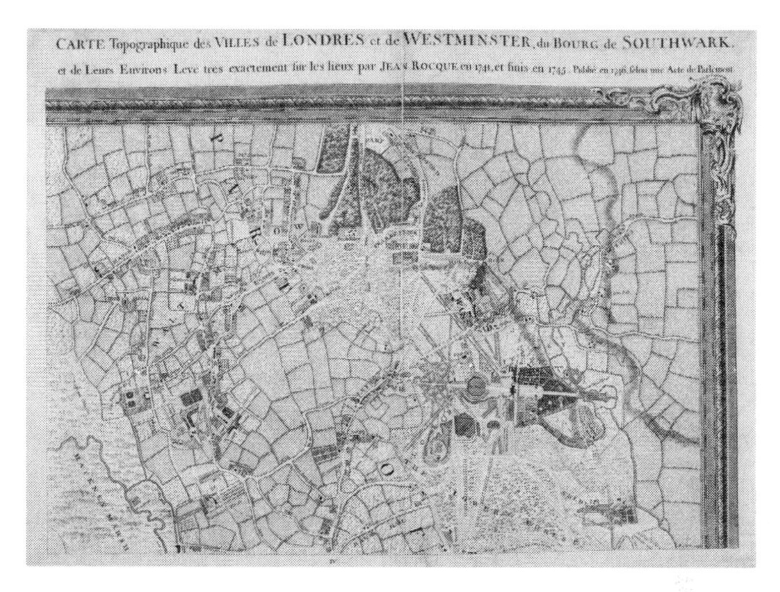

A glimpse of Walthamstow in John Roque's map of London and Essex, 1744. (Courtesy of London Metropolitan Archives)

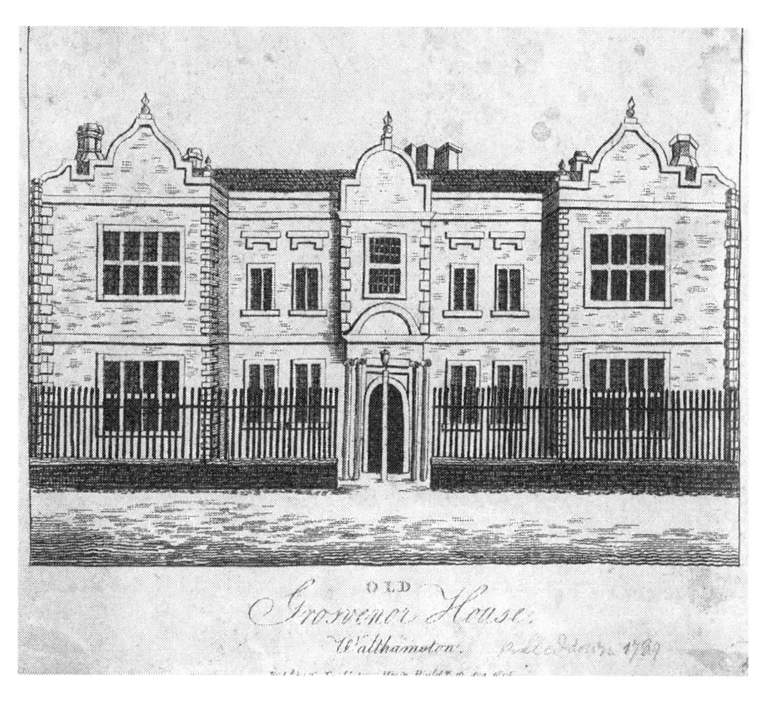

Grosvenor House was one of the grand mansions built in Hoe Street in the eighteenth century. (Reproduced by courtesy of Essex Record Office)

turned two pairs of stones in the presses. But by the nineteenth century a new scale of industry had arrived. In 1806 the British Copper Company had bought the site, installing a rolling mill, hammer mill and crane house. The copper company was publicly limited, raising capital from shareholders and investors, including Samuel Bosanquet, the Lord of Low Hall Manor, and integrated the mills into a national production chain transporting copper ingots by sea barge from smelting works near Swansea and up the Lea Navigation waterway. At the mills the ingots were rolled into sheets, which from 1812 to 1814 were sent up to the workshops of Birmingham to make tokens issued because of shortages in coinage. By 1824 around 84 tonnes of sheet copper were made each month.

Waterpower rather than steam power drove the machinery at the mills. In the 1830s the new owners raised the sill of a nearby weir to improve the head of water for the copper mill, flooding the adjoining lands and irritating the owners of the mills in Tottenham, who found their waterpower had been dropping drastically. It was estimated that the power generated by the stream turning the waterwheel was equal to a 20hp steam engine, which, while less reliable, was far cheaper. The huge expense of installing a steam engine meant that waterpower was still being used at the copper mills almost until the site closed in 1858.

The copper mills were a housing colony in the parish. A supervisor lived in comfort in a furnished house within the grounds, which was also used as administrative offices and a counting house, while the coppersmiths and their families lived in cottages which, by the 1840s, were housing more than fifty or so people. General labourers at the mills lived in the courts and yards at the lower end of Marsh Street, such as Paradise Row, Lilley's Yard and Ormes Row.

While young lads worked as labourers at the mills there was growing opposition to the employment of children in certain trades, particularly chimney sweeping. By the late eighteenth century homes and workshops were burning more coal and master chimney sweeps in London and elsewhere were employing boys as young as 7 or 8, whom they sent up the flues to clean out the soot, exposing the children to great danger, injury and sometimes even death. Benjamin Meggott Forster, whose family had owned Cleveland House in Hoe Street, was a member of the Committee to Promote the Superseding of Climbing Boys and campaigned for Parliament to ban the practice. Forster had probably heard about the London climbing boy who had to be rescued from the chimney of a carpenter's shop in Marsh Street in 1808, which featured in the campaigners' pamphlets exposing the horrors of the trade.

In Walthamstow, Forster and supporters of the committee encouraged residents to employ local tradesmen such as James Laver and George Turner who used the Scandiscope, a mechanical device operated with rods and brushes, which Forster used to clean a chimney in his home. Petitions were sent to Parliament and a public meeting held at the Chequers Inn on Marsh Street, heard from a master chimney sweep about the cruelty inflicted on the boys.

While there was concern about child labour in chimney sweeping and in the Lancashire cotton factories there was no general unease about children starting work at a young age. In Walthamstow many of the children of the labouring poor would have been expected to work and many probably did so until the start of elementary education with the opening of a National School at Church End in 1819. At the same time dissenting congregations organised their own British Schools in Marsh Street and Wood Street to help teach reading, writing and arithmetic. Most children were not as fortunate as the young Benjamin Disraeli, who attended Cogan's school for the sons of gentleman in Higham Hill, or the scholars at the Forest School, a fee-paying institution near Whipps Cross. Nor were they as lucky as William Morris, who was born in 1834 at Elm House on Clay Street and was tutored by the Reverend Dr Frederick Barlow Guy at his house in Hoe Street to help prepare him for entry to Oxford University in 1851. By then the wealthy Morris family had moved to the Winns, or the Water House as it was then called, the home of today's William Morris Gallery, where he had the leisure time to sit on a window seat of the grand staircase and read a book.

The abolition of child labour wasn't the only campaign supported by the people of Walthamstow during the Industrial Revolution – they also agitated against the horrors of slavery and the international slave trade. The wealthy Quaker David Barclay, of Marsh Street, freed the thirty-two slaves he had been left as a result of a debt on a farm in Jamaica from 1795, and campaigned for parliamentary legislation to end the trade in human chattel. Women were strongly involved in the cause. By the 1850s a Walthamstow Ladies' Anti-Slavery Association had organised an anti-slavery lecture every year and circulated abolitionist books and papers, as well as making 'articles of fancy' to be sold at fundraising bazaars which were held on both sides of the Atlantic.

But the biggest mobilisation of people was for political reform. When the 1832 Reform Act was passed just 121 wealthy men in Walthamstow were given the franchise, because to be on the register for Essex meant meeting one of the county property qualifications: freehold land with a rentable value of 40 shillings a year, paying an annual rent of £50 or more, copyhold land worth £10, or owning property of at least £10 a year rental value. No woman could vote.

Chartists were active in Walthamstow. The Chartist movement campaigned for the Six Points of the People's Charter: universal suffrage, the secret ballot, abolition of the voting property qualification, annual parliaments, equal representation and payment of MPs. In Walthamstow the main organiser was William James Linton, a wood engraver who lived in Woodford and who wrote articles and poems in the Radical newspapers under the pen name Spartacus. On 18 April 1839, as the Chartists' National Convention gathered in London, Linton arranged for two Chartist missionaries, Robert Knox and Richard Marsden, to speak at a public meeting. According to *The Charter*, the meeting supported setting up a Walthamstow Working Men's Association, and passed motions condemning the government for the poor's misery in strong language. 'This meeting is convinced that government, as at present constituted, is framed for the benefit of only a small portion of the community, and that the continual misery and consequent crimes of the laboring poor are mainly owing to the gross injustice of those who are called their betters,' it read.

The parish's well-to-do were horrified by what they viewed as seditious activity in the parish and Linton was stopped from using any hall or meeting venue. So, when he organised a public meeting for 1 May 1839 to support the National Petition, for which handbills were printed in London by the Radical printer James Watson, the people who turned up from Walthamstow, Leyton and other areas were forced to assemble at a clearing in the forest at Whipps Cross. Linton chaired the public meeting by clambering on to the stump of a felled tree.

But the middle classes in Walthamstow supported political reform. They had their own causes, which were also supported by the Chartists, such as the Corn Laws or the Bread Tax, for artificially raising prices by imposing tariffs on imported grain to help protect England's agriculture. A draper named Ebenezer Clarke, who lived in Marsh Street, founded a branch of the Anti-Corn Law Association, which met at the lecture hall in Wood Street, and collected signatures with his son Ebenezer demanding a repeal of the laws.

As a Presbyterian and leader of the dissenting community, Ebenezer Clarke had opposed compulsory church rates (his home on Marsh Street was called Voluntary House) and was fined after refusing to pay the churchwardens. It was a stance supported by Linton, whom Clarke now helped to set up

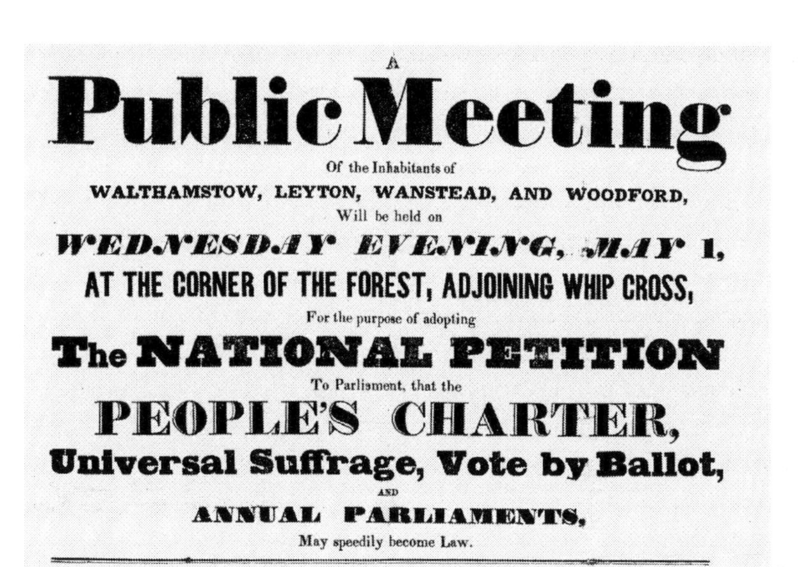

A
Public Meeting
Of the Inhabitants of
WALTHAMSTOW, LEYTON, WANSTEAD, AND WOODFORD,
Will be held on
WEDNESDAY EVENING, MAY 1,
AT THE CORNER OF THE FOREST, ADJOINING WHIP CROSS,
For the purpose of adopting
The NATIONAL PETITION
To Parliament, that the
PEOPLE'S CHARTER,
Universal Suffrage, Vote by Ballot,
AND
ANNUAL PARLIAMENTS,
May speedily become Law.

THE CHAIR WILL BE TAKEN AT HALF-PAST SIX PRECISELY.
Watson, Printer, 18, City Road, London.

Chartist handbill printed by Watson and distributed by Linton in 1839 to Walthamstow's residents. (Courtesy of the National Archives)

the Walthamstow Mutual Instruction Society, after establishing it had no illegal intentions, by allowing it to use the British School's rooms in Wood Street. Linton's political activities didn't make him popular among the City gentlemen with whom he travelled every day by coach from Woodford to his workshop in Hatton Garden. He recalled:

> My companions outside the coach were city men, bankers, and the like, whose residences were on the forest side. It was very long before I had so much as a 'good-morning' from them. The only offence I gave my neighbours was that I opposed the church-rates, and was known to be a Chartist.

Linton set up the Mutual Instruction Society as a meeting place to bring together people of all social classes and to aid political reform by improving the education of working people. He kept the subscription low at 6 shillings a year, so even the poorest could attend his lectures on slavery and temperance or read books from a library managed by the secretary Walter Whittingham, a master at the British School. Topics such as phrenology, the death penalty and the Corn Laws were discussed. 'I there gave my first lecture "Against

Death Punishment", and for the sake of the funds of the society, engaged in a three nights' discussion with a pious temperance preacher, who did not compliment me,' Linton remembered.

By the late 1840s the Walthamstow Mutual Instruction Society was still functioning even though its founder, William James Linton, had moved out of Essex. Chartism was fading but the spirit of political reform lived on in new organisations, which encouraged working men to gain the vote by purchasing enough freehold land to meet the property qualifications for the franchise, and Walthamstow was one of the places where they were the most active.

7

Land Societies, Philanthropy and Reform in the Railway Age

In the 1850s a vision of Walthamstow as a suburb for enfranchised artisans independent of the landowners was promoted by social reformers, who developed estates of freehold housing which challenged the old guard's domination of a parish still anchored in rural traditions with a socially select air.

The development was led by freehold land societies. They first started in 1847 when a nonconformist minister named James Taylor set up the Birmingham Freehold Land Society to secure the vote for working men by allowing them to buy a plot of land which met the 40-shilling freehold property qualification. Taylor, who was a temperance advocate, also believed the land society was a way to promote self-help, sobriety and thrift by encouraging working people to save money to obtain a plot of land. The largest of these organisations was the National Freehold Land Society, which was founded in 1849 at a meeting in London addressed by Richard Cobden MP, who, like other Radical Liberals, strongly supported the societies as a way of implanting freeholder voters in the rural counties where the Tory-inclined landlords often held sway over their tenants.

The society acquired freehold land in Walthamstow with the help of the now retired draper Ebenezer Clarke, his son Ebenezer junior, who had become a local agent for the society, and Walter Whittingham, its first full-time secretary. The first estate was 8 acres of parkland off Hoe Street purchased from Joseph Truman, who owned Grosvenor House opposite, which it bought in 1851 for £2,524. The National Freehold Land Society expanded rapidly in the early 1850s. It snapped up land on the old common off Markhouse Lane in 1852, 13 acres of the old Church Common in 1853, and an estate off Hoe Street. A fifth estate of 4 acres at Whipps Cross was bought in 1855, amounting to more than 38 acres of freehold land in the parish by the late 1850s.

The land societies operated in a similar way to building societies. A society acquired land, often with the help of a patron, and divided the estate into plots. Members paid in a minimum of 1*s* a week until they reached £30 and became full shareholders who could choose an allotment of freehold land from any estate owned by the society. The order for who chose first was decided by lot. They also had a self-help ethos. Members who wanted to build their own houses were encouraged to buy manuals such as *The Builder's Practical Director* or read the guidance on house building published in the society's journal, *The Freeholder's Circular*, which offered advice on everything from digging trenches to mixing concrete and different types of brick bonds.

The National wasn't the only freehold land society in the parish. By the 1850s there were sixty active in London, representing all shades of political opinion. In Walthamstow, the City of London and the St Pancras district, societies were buying up land and one of the largest was the Tower Hamlets Freehold Land Society, which bought a large estate at Parsonage Hill, off Green Leaf Lane in 1854. It pegged out 425 allotments of land, acquired by tradesmen and working people from Bethnal Green who built their own cottages, and also laid out Byron Road, Brown's Road, Tower Hamlets Road, Aubrey Road and Milton Road.

The National was very thorough in preparing each estate for building. A surveyor was appointed to draw up a plan and lay out the freehold plots and roads, and a clerk of the works oversaw the filling in of ditches and digging out of tree roots before the ground was cleared and levelled. Gravel was spread as a road surface and road drains, gulley gratings, and cast-iron pipes were installed to provide drainage. Fencing was put up around each plot and deeds printed. The estates were laid out with new streets. On the old Markhouse Common they drew up Prospect Terrace, Union Road and Prospect Road, while on the old Church Common houses were laid out on Beulah Road and Eden Road. At the Grosvenor estate, the long straight Grosvenor Park Road was laid out where the avenue of elms which once stood on Truman's parkland had been hacked down.

Milton Road was one of the streets laid out by the Tower Hamlets Freehold land society. (Courtesy of Vestry House Museum, London Borough of Waltham Forest)

As a largely rural area, Walthamstow was very attractive to working people from London who hoped to acquire property by joining a land society. The *Freeholders Land Times*, in a write-up about the National's estate at Grosvenor Park, said while the cutting down of the old avenue of elm trees had been a mistake by the society, the development had been to a high standard and noted the 'land around is well-cultivated and extremely fertile and this with the natural climate renders the air of Walthamstow bracing and healthy'.

Relationships between the members were not always fraternal. In 1857 at Church Common, a blacksmith from Whitecross Street in the capital named Stephen Million had marked out his plot with a wooden fence. He later found that the owner of the neighbouring plot, a carpenter named Alfred London, had ripped out the fencing and wooden posts to use the wood for scaffolding and to support the doors and windows inside the two houses he was building with his workmen. The two men had earlier fallen out over water being run on to Million's land. There were threats of a case at the county court. The carpenter was later arrested and prosecuted, but acquitted of stealing the wood.

There were often tensions in the leadership of the National. In 1854 Ebenezer Clarke was accused of wrongdoing by Edwin Mantz, who lived in South Grove and was a former Chartist. Mantz accused Clarke of enriching himself with the purchases made in Walthamstow, turning up at a meeting of the society with a report of Clarke's supposed crimes, and accused Clarke of 'finding, buying, surveying many valuable estate and appropriating the cream of everything to himself'. Mantz also made rumblings that Clarke's son, who was a local agent, earned a commission on sales of land.

The development of the estates by the land societies contributed to population growth, which rose from a recorded 4,959 in 1851 to 7,144 in 1861. But as the younger Ebenezer Clarke noted, many of the gentry and local well-to-do in Walthamstow were unhappy with the arrival of working people into the area, which they hoped to preserve as a rural suburb with a select air.

The elite clung on to their old traditions. The Court Leet of Walthamstow Toni still took place at the Ferry Boat Inn near the bridge on the boundary with Tottenham every Whitsun Tuesday to elect ale-conners and constables and to deal with the admission of heirs to their estates and the transfer of property. Parish dinners were still enjoyed at the inn near the Lea with singing, drinking and feasting and were hosted by a Mr Nokes, who had a hook instead of a hand.

In 1867, the beating of the bounds was carried out by almost 200 people on foot, with bell-ringers and a drum and flute band. The churchwardens and beadle led the procession around the boundaries marked by wooden posts, which were symbolically whacked with willow wands. There could be confusion in trying to remember exactly where some of the boundaries were, especially as the ceremony was carried out infrequently and vestry officials in Tottenham pulled up the markers where Walthamstow had parcels of land on their side of the Lea. But it was enjoyable. At the vestry's expense, those perambulating the bounds paused at the Ferry Boat for beer and bread and cheese, and at the end of the day enjoyed a good supper at the Nag's Head and more pots of beer.

However, the land societies were upsetting the political balance of the area. By 1861, 203 of the 402 men on the Essex county register for Walthamstow had qualified for the vote as 40-shilling freeholders, and at general elections in the late 1850s the Walthamstow division of the South Essex seat started to swing to the Liberals, which no doubt was welcomed by Edward Lloyd, the Radical publisher and owner of *Lloyd's Weekly*, who moved into the Water House in 1857. The elder Clarke and Walter Whittingham still fought the old nonconformist causes by challenging the church rates and election of churchwardens at vestry meetings, but were defeated by plural voting each time.

The Clarkes fused philanthropic principles with developing their own housing. At Stratford, Clarke senior had built fifty cottages by 1862, which were let at 3*s* 6*d* a week and returned a net profit of 5 per cent, while his son was active in the Central Cottage Improvement Society, which promoted the building of model housing by landlords who let property at reasonable rents but still made a sound return for the capitalist. The Clarkes were 'five per cent philanthropists'. To promote its work the society exhibited a life-size model cottage at the South Kensington International Exhibition in 1862. And it appears to have been that model which Ebenezer Clarke junior appears to have chosen when he built his own model cottages in Walthamstow. He bought freehold building plots and built eighteen model cottages on Eden Road costing £170 each. They were built in pairs and had separate front doors but the appearance of one building, as can still be seen today. The local building firm of Anthony Storey Reed, with whom the Clarkes were on good terms, may well have built the cottages.

The model cottages were popular. Clarke junior claimed to have advertised in *Lloyd's Weekly* on a Saturday and by the Monday there were ninety applications for the cottages, mainly from people living in Spitalfields in East London. They were let to families at 3*s* 6*d* a week, bringing in an income of £234 a year, and Clarke also offered a mortgage arrangement for artisans to pay 5*s* a week. The cottages were a vast improvement on most working people's housing with a parlour, sitting room, two bedrooms, wash-house, oven and a range, as well as a garden for growing fruit and vegetables, and were far cheaper than renting in London.

Clarke junior believed that his cottages in Walthamstow, built on a philanthropic model, offered a solution to the metropolis's housing crisis. He set out his vision of Walthamstow as a suburb for the sturdy and independent artisan in *The Hovel and the Home*, which was aimed at philanthropic landlords, working people and artisans in East London who wished to build their own homes outside the capital and escape the smoky, overcrowded courtyards of Spitalfields. He claimed that his houses would offer:

> A garden where children could breathe the fresh air, smell the sweet perfume of rose and honey-suckle; instead of husband being driven to the public house, he is glad to return to his family, employ himself with his children in attending to flowers and vegetables.

But not everybody welcomed this development. As Clarke pointed out, there were plenty of rural cottages in a decayed state but many of the owners

Ebenezer Clarke built a model cottage to this design at Eden Road in Walthamstow. (Courtesy of Mary Evans Picture Library)

were more interested in building kennels for their hounds than high-quality housing for tenants. Members of the local gentry objected to Clarke's building of homes for working people and threatened to leave the parish, fearing that the rural character was being destroyed and that the poor rates would rise. But that didn't stop the societies or the Clarkes. By 1861, a total of 545 houses had been built on estates belonging to the land societies, including fifty-eight properties off Markhouse Lane, twenty in Orford Road, and thirteen cottages in Eden Road.

Clarke extended philanthropy beyond housing. The supply of water was still primitive in many parts of Walthamstow. People mainly fetched water from a public well and even the grander houses in Grosvenor Park Road, where the Clarkes had a house, shared a private dipper well. Clarke was one of those who supported a fund set up by the Barclay family to build a pump in the poorest part of Wood Street called Jeffries Square, not far from the house where Joseph Jeffreys had been murdered.

Philanthropists were also instrumental in setting up the St James's Club at Lower Marsh Street in 1862. The area had been growing because of the copper mills and a brewery opened by William Hawes, and in 1842 a chapel called St James's opened. Part of Marsh Street from St James's Church to Markhouse Lane become known as St James Street. The St James's Club, which later changed its name to the Walthamstow Working-Men's Club and Institute, was supported by Clarke and other philanthropists including

Barclay's Pump was installed in Jefferies Square at Wood Street. (Courtesy of Vestry House Museum, London Borough of Waltham Forest)

Markhouse Lane in the 1860s, not far from the old Markhouse Common. (Courtesy of Vestry House Museum, London Borough of Waltham Forest)

Henry Solly. The rules banned 'smoking, singing and improper language' and it was open daily until 10 p.m. and cost 4*d* a month to join. Tea and coffee were served – it was a teetotal environment – and in the library the men could read the *Illustrated London News*, *Punch* and *Penny Post*, and play chess, draughts, dominoes and solitaire.

The railway was central to Clarke junior's vision because it offered the opportunity to work in London and travel to a model cottage in a suburb.

On the edge of the parish, Lea Bridge station had opened in 1840 on the line from London to Cambridge, which ran over a section of the old common marsh in Walthamstow, forcing the Northern and Eastern Railway to compensate those who lost common grazing rights on the old lammas meadows.

Since the 1850s some major landowners had been campaigning for a direct railway. Other suburbs outside London had increased their land values with a direct rail route which offered gentleman an easy commute to the City. The old guard feared Walthamstow would become a working-class suburb if a rail link opened; however, two bills were presented to Parliament in 1864 for competing routes. There was a proposal by the Walthamstow, Clapton and City Railway and a separate plan by the Great Eastern Railway, which was accepted by MPs, for a route from a new station to be built at Liverpool Street up to Chingford, which would run parallel with Marsh Street and have new stops at St James Street, Hoe Street and Wood Street.

Construction on the line to Walthamstow started in 1866. At St James Street, a station was completed and the track had been laid by 1867, but the Great Eastern ran out of funds and the work stopped. Landowners with capital tied up in estate and housing development offered to help financially. Work restarted and the workmen dug a cutting through Church Common for which, in compensation, the vestry was given funds to buy a recreation ground for Walthamstow's people – it bought a field off Selbourne Road.

As the railway bills were debated in the House of Commons, the MPs slipped in an amendment that workmen's tickets would be available on trains to Walthamstow before 7 a.m. and after 6 p.m. at a penny fare or 2*d* return to compensate for the demolition of working-class housing around Liverpool Street. Working people wanted a railway to Walthamstow and campaigned for cheaper fares. A Mr Elverton, who had relocated his family from Bethnal Green, spoke at public meetings, calling for railway companies to run workmen's trains until 8 a.m. and complaining that he was forced to walk 72 miles a week to the dockyards in London because the railway was so expensive.

In spring 1870 the Great Eastern suddenly decided to open a spur line running from Lea Bridge station ahead of the agreed line from Liverpool Street to Chingford, which was still being completed, through Walthamstow. There were no timetables, name boards at the stations or clocks on the platforms, but inspectors agreed it could open. The railway was coming to Walthamstow.

8

Railway Suburb: Builders, Terraces and Timetables

On 23 April 1870 a steam locomotive pulling carriages chugged out of Lea Bridge station, trundled along a new track laid over the meadows and marshland and stopped at St James Street, then Hoe Street station before terminating at a temporary station which had been built near to Shernhall Street.

The first trains to Walthamstow were a shuttle service on the one-track spur running to Lea Bridge and from there passengers had to change for a train to Stratford and then connect to another train before arriving at Bishopsgate. It took until 1872 for Great Eastern to run timetabled trains every half hour, but even then it could still be a chaotic experience and a letter to the *Walthamstow Chronicle*, which printed the timetables in full, complained of passenger scrums at Stratford and having to travel in the guards' brake because of the packed-out trains, which sometimes terminated at Fenchurch Street rather than Bishopsgate station. In 1873 a station north of Hale End was opened, which was called Highams Park, and a newly built station at Wood Street replaced the temporary stop at Shernhall Street and the branch line from Liverpool Street to Chingford was opened.

Hoe Street was the busiest stop. The stationmaster rang a bell when the trains were approaching, sending people running down the paths from all around to catch the service. When Hoe Street station first opened there was only one station building on the 'up' side of the tracks amid the fields. Later when the building on the 'down' side opened, those returning to Walthamstow from London had to squeeze up a flight of stairs and file across a bridge between the platforms in order to leave, waiting in the icy wind for their tickets to be inspected.

Among the crowds streaming towards Hoe Street in the 1870s to catch the first 'up' train to London in the morning were artisans, clerks and working people, with many of the men wearing boots, corduroy jackets and aprons, and holding tool bags. At the station ticket office, they would have presented a certificate signed by their employer, which entitled them to the workman's fare of 1*d* for a single ticket or 2*d* return on weekdays. The ticket was only valid on the day of issue and there was no return until after 4 p.m. In 1874, even a third-class season ticket from Hoe Street was as much as 13*s* 6*d* a month, and required a deposit of 2*s* 6*d*. But the workmen's fare encouraged large numbers to head to Hoe Street and St James Street stations in the morning. The British Workman public house seized the commercial opportunity and opened at 4.30 a.m. to serve the hungry travellers food and beer.

Hoe Street Station in the early twentieth century. (Courtesy of Vestry House Museum, London Borough of Waltham Forest)

Inside a workman's train in late nineteenth-century London. (*Illustrated London News*, Mary Evans Picture Library)

The numbers travelling on the railway line rapidly increased. By 1882, Great Eastern Railway estimated that 2,333 workmen were travelling from Hoe Street station each week, and 2,694 from St James Street. The company wasn't always keen on workmen's tickets and there were complaints that ticket holders were barred from third-class, and clapped-out carriages were run on the early trains. At Liverpool Street the company attempted to separate the workmen from the 'respectable' passengers, claiming that many smoked, spat and left the platforms so filthy that ladies avoided walking on them. But many MPs supported cheaper tickets for working people and the company was running three half-fare trains a day to Walthamstow by the 1880s.

The cheap workman's tickets on early morning trains tempted working-class families to Walthamstow. On the estate built by the Tower Hamlets Freehold Land Society the population was said to have doubled in the early 1870s and on Aubrey Road a cottage was let for as little as 5*s* a week in 1874. According to a letter in *The Builder*, the new arrivals, who took trains to London from Hoe Street station a short walk away, brought in lodgers and two families often 'doubled up', sharing one house together. A few kept their own pigs as well. The writer also claimed that on the other side of Parsonage Hill to the Tower Hamlets estate had appeared large houses 'of a very pretentious character'. These were detached villas built as part of the Prospect Hill Park Estate. These villas were neo-Gothic in design with elaborate porticos, terracotta arched recesses, front gardens, kitchens, and separate rooms for servants. They were for sale or rent to the upper middle-classes, who commuted to London by train and wanted a comfortable home in a salubrious suburb to return to at night. This was the other side of the housing boom triggered by the railway.

The thought of easy profits encouraged speculative builders to put up new houses. Journeymen who often had little previous building experience or knowledge switched into the industry because credit was easy to get and land plentiful. A speculative builder usually worked ahead of demand, borrowing from building societies and often buying materials from the builders' merchant on tick, and, as soon as the roof was on a property, it was sold or leased so he could pay the creditors. Some builders prospered, others speculated rashly and were ruined by a glut. It wasn't unusual to see houses standing empty for a few years in Walthamstow.

View from the tower of St Mary's in the 1870s, from which could be seen the railway cutting through Church End. (Courtesy of Vestry House Museum, London Borough of Waltham Forest)

There was even jerry-building. Walthamstow was outside the control of the Metropolitan Board of Works until 1887 and relied on local bylaws and a surveyor employed by the Local Board of Health to regulate building. A workman recalled that jerry-building was often a product of the builder's own struggle to survive in a cut-throat environment, as he was forced to scamp on the job to keep down his costs. Scams were feared, including moving stairs from one house to another soon after the surveyor had inspected or saving money by nailing floorboards on one side and every other joist. In 1880 four houses built by Frederick Johnson on Marsh Street partly collapsed because the party walls were too thin and the bricks and mortar had not set properly due to the hasty work. Embarrassingly for the Board, the surveyor, Mr Swan, had inspected the building during the works and Johnson's plans had been submitted. It followed a previous house collapse in the same area.

There were, however, many good craftsmen working in the building trade, which in the 1870s was becoming one of the leading industries in Walthamstow. The best small masters grew quickly. In the 1860s Good Brothers was founded by Edward Good, who had trained as a carpenter and migrated as a young man from the town of Coggeshall in rural Essex to Walthamstow, setting up his workshop with his brother. He was dedicated and hard-working enough to succeed against competition in the trade. Good was ascetic, he ate two meals a day and abstained from alcohol, waking up at 5 a.m. every day with a clear-head, and would stay on a job until late, watching his tradesmen like a hawk.

The greatest demand was for two-storey terraced houses and they mushroomed on the common lands and around St James Street, where a house with a parlour room, which was the dream of many working-class families migrating up from London, could be rented for just 11*s* a week. The terraces spread across Higham Hill, which had escaped development on the old common in the 1860s, as St Andrew's Road, Mayfield Road, Oatland Rise, Mount Pleasant Road and other roads were started in the 1870s. Probably the most unusual name was Master McGrath Terrace in Shernhall Street, which was christened in honour of the Irish greyhound Master McGrath, winner of the Waterloo Cup in 1868, 1869 and 1871, and a favourite with punters.

House building triggered a surge in brickmaking at Chapel End and other rural areas. Brickfields making as many as 900 bricks an hour were founded by Mr Stotter, Edwin Barltrop, and Eli Wilson. Wilson's in Billet Lane opposite Moons Farm was probably the biggest operation, bringing

Gregory's at Wood Street was one of the many brickfields in the 1880s. (Courtesy of Vestry House Museum, London Borough of Waltham Forest)

in men from Kent and housing them in cottages nearby in what was still an isolated rural area even after the railway opened. But the competition was fierce. One of the brick-makers in 1883 slashed his piece rates by 6*d* per 1,000 bricks, which threatened a substantial drop in pay for the workers and provoked a strike by hundreds of men, which reversed the cut.

Chapel End was still one of the rural areas in the 1880s, despite the arrival of the railway. There were still a number of farms, including Moons Farm in Billet Lane, Salisbury Hall Farm at the site of the old manor house, and Wadham Farm. Many of them supplied milk and dairy products to the growing population of London. Bulls Farm was still operating in Higham Hill on the eve of the Great War. The Great Eastern Railway liked to play up Walthamstow's rural character in the 1880s, printing in its guidebooks that the area was 'remarkable for its picturesque and well-timber undulations' and portraying it as a place of mansions, comfortable middle-class housing and artisans' homes.

Old rural traditions were no longer respected as they had been in the past. At Low Hall Farm, the new tenant farmer shut an old footpath across the fields from the old common at Markhouse Lane to Lea Bridge Road, erecting a 'Trespassers Will Be Prosecuted' sign. A public meeting was called at the

The Blue Cottages on Blackhorse Lane, pictured in 1900, were survivors of older housing in Walthamstow. (Courtesy of Vestry House Museum, London Borough of Waltham Forest)

Agriculture survived in some areas such as Bull's Farm in Higham's Hill, where they were loading the hay in 1912. (Courtesy of Vestry House Museum, London Borough of Waltham Forest)

Common Gate pub in protest and to put pressure on the Local Board, which now owned the land, but the farmer was unmoved and the way stayed shut.

There was a growing reaction against the juggernaut of rows of terraced housing and brickfields rolling over the old fields. The old guard complained that urbanisation had triggered a social decline, transforming a once-genteel suburb into an East End slum. 'Poor Walthamstow has fallen into evil days,' lamented a letter in the *Walthamstow Guardian*. 'The aggressive builder has converted many of the fair fields into foul brickyards and hewn down the noble monarchs of a former forest with the barbarous zeal of a vandal.' They were particularly disturbed by the destruction of the grand houses with their avenues of trees, pleasure grounds and gardens. In 1883 The Cedars, a large house on Hoe Street, which had been the home of Alfred Janson, was pulled down after his death and laid out as building plots. In a final act of desecration, the floorboards, doors and pipes were auctioned off as building materials, and a splendid row of ornamental trees were felled. In its place was built the Cedars Estate, with names such as Shrubland Road and Sylvan Road hinting at a rural past and rows of 'villas' with ornate painted porches.

William Morris was appalled by the destruction of the area's rural heritage and was saddened that the Walthamstow he remembered from his childhood had been choked up by terraces which were 'cocknified' or cocksure in taste. Others agreed. At the turn of the century John Mackail, Morris's friend and official biographer, complained that Walthamstow was dominated by 'rows of flimsily built two-storey houses in all the hideousness of yellow brick and blue slate'.

There were mutterings about the spread of the terraced 'villas'. One local newspaper felt that no housing built quickly to be rented out to working-class tenants or clerks for as little as 6*s* 6*d* a week could be described as a 'villa'. After another jerry-building scare in 1887, an editorial in the *Walthamstow Express* didn't hold back. It stated what many of the well-to-do felt about the 'villas' which were being erected across the suburb where the grand houses had once stood, arguing that a villa was 'something poor and pretentious' and all show.

The landowners as well as builders developed housing in the new suburb. One of Walthamstow's largest landowners in the 1880s was Theydon Courtenay Warner, whose huge family estate included the manor of Higham Benstead, purchased by an ancestor, as well as land in East Anglia and elsewhere. Warner owned a lot of land at the lower end of Marsh Street, including the Clock House, a grand mansion set in large grounds built by his grandfather Thomas Courtenay Warner in 1813, which happily survives to this day.

By the time the railway to Walthamstow opened the Warners had set out to redevelop their estates as housing and had left the Clock House for the splendid Highams House, a manor house rebuilt in the eighteenth century set in landscaped grounds near Woodford. The Clock House was leased out to tenants. Warner had plans for developing his estate on a large scale. In 1887 the chairman of the Local Board, William Whittingham, a son of Walter Elliott Whittingham, and the new surveyor met John Dunn, an architect employed by the Warner estate, to discuss plans for a development of the Clock House area. Dunn drafted and submitted proposals for an estate including streets called Pretoria Avenue, Warner Road, Chewton Road, Northcote Road, Maud Road and Maud Terrace; all of the names had a connection with the Warner family, which were passed by the Board of Health as being suitable the next year.

Warner's estate was completely different to anything else which had been built in Walthamstow. Speculative builders had laid out small clumps of terraced houses and often streets were completed at different times by a series of different builders. But the Clock House estate, which preserved the old house, was radically different because Warner set up his own company to build houses directly rather than rely on signing building leases, which he had done in the past to develop his estate. The straight tree-lined roads had excellent sanitation and drainage for the time and the company built red-brick maisonette houses, designed by Dunn, as well as a small number of larger houses, often using high-quality materials. The maisonettes with their own front doors and patch of garden at the back were designed to attract the sorts of artisan and lower-middle class 'respectable' tenants who Warner hoped would flock to the Clock House and the company's other estates, such as the Winns at Chapel End, which was built later.

Warner's were innovative in their use of advertising to attract potential tenants from across the capital when the Clock House had been finished in the 1890s. They took out adverts in the London daily newspapers, which presented the estate as a prestigious development built in a pleasant suburb where one could live 'Well and Cheaply, Hale and Hearty' and travel to the capital easily. Warner's were fastidious in keeping their estate spick-and-span and only allowed the doors and woodwork to be painted in the regulation cream and green paint, which can still be glimpsed on a handful of the houses today.

However, Courtenay Warner's motives were not just about development. He was also politically ambitious. In 1889 he was elected to Essex County Council for the St James district of Walthamstow and was determined to become a Liberal MP, eventually securing a constituency in the West Country. He courted working-class voters by announcing he was a Radical who supported one-man-one-vote, free education and even a tax on ground rent, which was quite surprising given the scale of his landholdings and

Warner Estates advertised their properties in the newspapers. (Courtesy of the British Library and Solo Syndication, *London Daily News*)

property. In 1892 as building of the Clock House estate was under way, Warner met the Operative Bricklayers' Society branch secretary at the Workman's Hall, who was complaining about some of the subcontractors working on the scheme, to pledge that every worker would be paid a fair wage on the job. Warner and his wife, Lady Leucha, were forever attending openings and charity events to ensure that he maintained a high profile as a leading citizen of the area.

It wasn't just houses which the growing suburb needed. In 1880 a School Board for Walthamstow was founded to organise compulsory schooling for all children in the parish aged 5 to 14 and it quickly began a building programme. Higham Hill School was built in 1883 followed by Marsh Street Boys and Pretoria Avenue in 1888. The red-brick Board schools towered over the terraces of new housing – the largest educated 1,198 scholars – and were far bigger than even the National School which had opened in Orford Road in 1866. The older schools were being redeveloped as well as their pupils increased, and in 1889 the Monoux school left the gallery room above the almshouses and moved into new buildings at the top of the High Street.

The building of new places of worship reflected Walthamstow's changing population. In the 1870s Primitive Methodists had started to hold open-air meetings in Marsh Street, on the Tower Hamlets estate and at Markhouse Common. They were led by Thomas Jackson, superintendent of the Bethnal Green Mission, who reached out to the downtrodden by visiting people's homes and lodging houses, offering breakfasts at Sunday services and running soup kitchens for the hungry. In 1893 the Methodists opened the Lighthouse Mission in Markhouse Road. The Lighthouse had originally been the site of tent meetings and a corrugated iron hut until the Methodist ship owner Captain King funded the new building, which had a turret with a revolving light beaming out during the Sunday service to guide in the people.

The Salvation Army also worked amongst the outcast. In 1888 Captain Hannah Slater started a marquee campaign to reach out to the most downtrodden of Walthamstow's new population. The Army first operated from an iron hut on the High Street, known as the Glory Shop, until a citadel was built in the 1890s. They held parades to announce their presence in the area. A brass band made up of the newest converts led the marchers. Most of them had no musical training and played only to drown out the booing and hissing by toughs.

There was friction between many Methodists and the Salvationists, who strongly supported the Temperance Movement, and local breweries and pubs. Salvation Army members at times preached the gospel and teetotalism outside public houses, especially if they opened on Sundays, provoking the ire of publicans who encouraged thugs to attack them and grab the Army's colours. A growing number of teetotal working-men and women wouldn't go in pubs. By the 1890s the Samson Lodge of the Sons of Phoenix met at Markhouse Common and the Horseshoe coffee tavern in St James Street, and for total abstainers and teetotalers there was also Ernest Rolfe's market stall in the High Street, which sold lemonade, sarsaparilla and coffee to quench a thirst.

Yet many did drink and in the 1880s new public houses were built for the growing population of Walthamstow including the Lorne Arms in Queens

Ernest Rolfe's stall on the High Street sold coffee, sarsaparilla and lemonade, and was popular with teetotallers. Ernest is to the right of Annie Rolfe. (Courtesy of Vestry House Museum, London Borough of Waltham Forest)

Road, Tower Hotel in Hoe Street (which was erected for Collier Brothers brewery who took over Hawes' brewery at James Street in 1871), and the Lord Brooke in Shernhall Street. There was a rebuilding of Walthamstow's older inns such as the Cock, and Coach and Horses in St James Street. Even the Chequers Inn, which was built in the eighteenth century, was spruced up.

Beer remained popular because of lingering concerns about safe drinking water. But a supply of piped water was being provided by the East London Water Works Company, which had taken over the copper mills and built water storage reservoirs, completing five by 1866, as well as a pumping station with an Italianate tower near Ferry Lane which pumped water from the reservoirs via an aqueduct to the filtering beds south of the Lea Bridge Road. In the 1870s, in what was a major engineering project, the company also completed the Racecourse Reservoir, High and Low Maynard Reservoirs, and the Warwick Reservoir to provide East London with a supply of piped water. The reservoirs were the sites of many archaeological discoveries from the late 1860s.

The Board of Health's Medical Officer Frederick Best used his new legal powers to compel landlords to connect their cottages to a supply of piped water. In 1876, when an old cottager complained of being made unwell by the water in a public well on Markhouse Lane, Best suspected typhoid and ordered it to be shut, sticking a notice on the well and filling it with gravel for good measure. Best told the owner, who happened to be Samuel Bosanquet, Lord of Low Hall Manor, to supply the cottages with piped water from the water company. Bosanquet was enraged. He insisted that the water in his wells was a pure natural supply and the cottager's illness 'inflammation of the bowels' and accused the Medical Officer publicly of working in the interests of a private company. Eventually, the medical officer won and the cottages were connected to piped water.

Best presented the Nuisances Committee of the Board of Health with the damning results of his investigation into the water supply for some old houses. On 23 June 1876, Best told the committee that there was hardly a pump in an area around Ormes Row and Saltwell's Yard off St James Street that was satisfactory. Most people relied on pumps to draw water up from a well, but he found that one of the pumps was drawing up water from a well near to a filthy stable and dung heap. Another supplying five houses was contaminated with sewage and unfit for use, and there was a pump contaminated by a pigsty and slaughterhouse near to it. The situation wasn't much better in the areas of old rural housing, where people drank brackish water from the forest which was sold on carts. Best tried to inform people of health risks, advising residents to test if their water from a cistern or water butt was safe by adding drops of Condy's Fluid to a sample in a glass and watch if the water turned pink.

The Nuisances Committee was kept busy as the worst sanitary and housing problems in the older country areas were reported. At Jeffries Square in the 1870s, not far from where Joseph Jeffreys house had stood, they were told of a privy emptying into a cesspool, untapped drains and tumbledown buildings, and conditions were just as bad at Budd's Alley in Wood Street and the old weather-boarded cottages in Blind Lane. Everywhere, open ditches used for sanitation along the sides of roads were filled in.

The Board of Health, set up in 1873 and elected by plural voting, struggled to cope with its responsibilities for maintaining the roads, rubbish collection, sanitation and nuisances as the population of Walthamstow grew rapidly. Board members, including Francis Wragg who had retired from his horse-drawn omnibus business in 1880, were perpetually worried about provoking a ratepayers' revolt by increasing the rates and billed the owners of property, regardless of their income, for improvement works to the roads or sanitation. This meant that it could take years for new sewers or sanitation works to be built. Nonetheless, the Board later built a sewage farm at Low Hall, which flushed the area's waste via the Dagenham Brook into the River Lea. The sewage farm had a pumphouse built in 1885 with the latest model of steam engines.

In a dizzying period of growth after the opening of the railway, Walthamstow's population increased to 22,531 people in 1881 and 47,154 in 1891, and during the 1890s the population continued to rise remorselessly. The distinctiveness of the old street-villages at Marsh Street, Clay Street and Wood Street disappeared as the fields which had separated these areas were built on. By the 1880s landowners sold up as the value of agricultural land – worth £150 per acre – sold at £1,200 per acre as building land.

The development had split the railway suburb into two socially distinctive camps by the 1890s. There was the old Walthamstow of long-established and largely well-to-do residents and their servants, tradesmen and farmers, as well as country folk and the odd City gentleman who were anchored in the traditions of the vestry and the parish church. The new Walthamstow was the world of the working-class operative, artisan and the clerk who lived in Warner estate housing or in the two-storey terraced houses in the urbanised areas of St James and the High Street. Most had not lived in Walthamstow for long. In the late 1880s, Jesse Argyle, a district visitor for Charles Booth, visited Walthamstow and walked around St James, which was brimming with 20,000 or so people and had been dubbed Little Bethnal Green because of the influx of East Enders. Argyle noted that while it had pockets of respectability with terraced streets occupied by policemen, postmen and clerks, there were the same signs of poverty he had seen in the East End of homes with broken windows filled up with rags, and ragged children playing in the streets.

There was tension between these two Walthamstows. Many of the new arrivals faced unemployment, overcrowded housing and poverty and disliked the way the old guard ran the vestry and Local Board. By the 1890s more of these people had won the vote. They were receptive to new political beliefs and now seized their opportunity to elect people who would represent them.

9

Dormitory Town: Radicals, Clerks and Costermongers

On a sunny day in May 1897, a procession set off promptly from Markhouse Common at 3 p.m. The thousands of marchers carried banners of temperance societies, including the Sons of Phoenix Samson Lodge, and trade unions were led by branches of the National Plate Glass Bevellers and the Operative Stone Masons. At the head of the parade was a large banner emblazoned with the words: 'To celebrate the victory of Mr Sam Woods the Labour and Progressive MP'.

In a carriage decorated with bunting and regalia sat the trade unionist and miners' leader from Lancashire, Mr Sam Woods, whom the people of Walthamstow had returned to Parliament as MP for the South-West Division of Essex. Following behind were decorated traps, carriages and a three-horse brake filled with aldermen, councillors and ladies and gentlemen representing nonconformist churches and chapels, and the Liberal and Radical Club. The procession, accompanied by a flying column of cyclists and brass bands, paraded around the streets of Walthamstow. Cheering crowds applauded Woods and men and women waved handkerchiefs from the windows of their houses, which were decorated with bunting and regalia.

But not everyone was celebrating. Many of the shopkeepers in St James Street and the High Street shut their stores for the day in protest and as the procession passed by a furniture shop the driver of a delivery cart blocked the path of the parade until the police moved him on. The parade was so large it took four hours to return to the common, where the speakers on different platforms relished Woods's political glory.

On 3 February that year Sam Woods, who stood as a Liberal and Radical candidate, beat the Conservative and Unionist Thomas Dewar in a historic by-election overturning a large Tory majority by 6,518 votes to 6,239 to became just one of a handful of working men to sit in the House of Commons. The constituency, which included Walthamstow, Leyton and Wanstead, had one of the largest electorates in the country, with 19,846 registered voters. Women still did not have the vote for parliamentary elections.

The candidates could not have been more different. Woods started life working in a pit as a pony driver aged 7 for 1 shilling a day. He learned to read and write at Sunday school and studied to become a Baptist minister. A lifelong teetotaler, he had risen through the ranks of the labour movement to become vice-president of the Miners' Federation of Great Britain. He had briefly been the MP for a mining constituency in Lancashire in the early 1890s. His opponent, Thomas Dewar, was the rich young director of his family's whisky business, Dewar's. He was a handsome and dashing young businessman who owned a stable of thoroughbred racehorses and a country seat in Kent. He had even written a book about his travels around the world promoting Dewar's whisky. When the campaign started, few gave Sam Woods a chance: Liberal candidates had been crushed at the last two elections for the seat.

Woods, who called himself an advanced Radical, worked hard, speaking at forty meetings a week with the support of leading trade unionists, including Tom Mann and the Battersea MP John Burns. Dewar's campaign was more leisurely. He drove himself to meetings in a four-in-hand carriage (his skill in handling the reins impressed quite a few working-men interested in horses), addressing audiences at ticket-only meetings at the Victoria Hall in Hoe Street or speaking at a venue in the City to some of the 2,000 or so 'out-voters', these were the non-residents who owned property in the constituency which entitled them to vote in the South-West Essex by-election. Dewar was confident because Walthamstow had plenty of working-class Tories, and he was extremely popular in the more select areas of Walthamstow. At the Elm House Conservative Club, thirteen cases of Dewar's whisky were ordered for the victory party.

Polling day was quiet until trains from Liverpool Street pulled in after 5 p.m. and the men rushed out to get to the polling stations before they closed at 8 p.m. At St James Street station Woods's election agents had carts, wagons, and horse and traps waiting outside to ferry his working-class supporters while at Hoe Street, where there were more clerks living, a similar armada of carriages decorated with the Tory Party's insignia was being directed by a gentleman on horseback. The scholars from the Board schools cheered for their candidate in the streets, and even dogs were said to be dressed up in the colours of red, white and blue for Dewar and orange for Woods.

That evening a huge crowd gathered outside the Town Hall, where the Post Office had installed an electric telegraph to communicate the result quickly. After many hours a figure appeared at a window and announced that Woods had won by 6,518 votes to 6,239; then Woods appeared to greet his delirious supporters. At the victory procession a few months later it was clear that expectations of Sam Woods MP among many of these voters remained sky-high.

The dramatic change in Walthamstow's population in the last decades of the nineteenth century had laid the foundations for Woods's historic victory. In 1894 Radical candidates won all six seats in St James ward and two seats in Higham Hill on the new Walthamstow Urban District Council, which had just taken over the powers of the Board of Health and most of the vestry's. The district council had no property qualifications and all men and women aged 21 and over could vote. And Woods's victory was no fluke. In spring 1897 a coalition of Liberals and Radicals, known as Progressives, won a majority on the council against their opponents the Moderates, a grouping of tradesmen, supporters of the Ratepayers' Association and members of Elm House Conservative Club. For the next two decades, power on the district council swung back and forth between the two rival blocs.

Local politics was fractious. A leading Progressive was the schoolteacher James McSheedy, who had challenged the running of the vestry and Local Board since the 1880s and delighted in making intemperate attacks on his political opponents. Poisonous pen portraits of his adversaries in the local Radical press soured the atmosphere. Unsurprisingly, district council committees and meetings at the Town Hall in Orford Road often degenerated into slanging matches between the rival sets of councillors.

Despite the unruly political atmosphere, the district council made progress in improving services. Lloyd Park opened in 1900 after Edward Lloyd's family gave the Water House and grounds to the people. The Public Baths in the High Street were opened in 1900 and the council built and operated its own electricity power station on Exeter Road and a network of municipal trams operating from a tram station on Chingford Road. Electric lights lit up the High Street.

But outside the Town Hall there were more radical voices who regarded parks and trams as mere tinkering and demanded more far-reaching measures to end people's chronic poverty, unemployment and overcrowded housing. In the 1890s at street corners and on Sundays at Markhouse Common appeared orators from the Social Democratic Federation (SDF) who would stand on a wooden platform with a red flag fluttering in the wind. The SDF were socialists and argued for a new society to benefit those who worked 'by hand or brain'. The Federation was small, but Walthamstow had a large branch whose members included Valentine 'Val' McEntee, a Dubliner by birth, and Charles and Benjamin Buck, who ran a printing plant, as well as many women including Helen Campbell.

SDF branch meetings, which were held at the Socialist Club in Markhouse Road, were said to be noisy affairs notorious for their din of yelping, squabbling and spouting during debates. But it wasn't a dour organisation. At the weekends members took the train up to Epping Forest for picnics or they relaxed at soirées held at the Workman's Hall in the High Street, at which they enjoyed a dinner, music and singing. There was even a brass band, which rehearsed two evenings a week.

The patch of open space known as Markhouse Common was Walthamstow's own speakers' corner in the 1890s. The SDF sent up some of their best orators from London, such as Harry Quelch, editor of the party's newspaper *Justice*, who spoke on the stump for two hours, warning the workers that they were 'mugs' and the 'political parties were the sharpers in a confidence trick'. The SDF wasn't the only organisation on the common trying to win people to their cause. Temperance campaigners warning of the demon drink and Evangelical preachers also spoke there, and people from the St James area would stroll up to the common to listen to the lecturing. There was competition between the groups for the best speaking spot. Once the SDF members jostled for a speaking pitch with a group of Evangelicals, who had attempted to drive off the socialists by standing a speaker with a booming voice on a platform just inches away from the rival orator.

Popular Conservatism was also a strong political force in Walthamstow. Elm House Conservative Club in the High Street had around 800 members, many of whom were working people, as well as the middle classes. But for many the club's billiard tables, well-stocked bar and concerts were as appealing as its political leanings and even the odd Radical was a member.

Many employers were Conservatives, as were publicans, who disliked the temperance leanings of the Liberals and Radicals. Shopkeepers were often Tories. Reuben Jolly, who built up Everett's into an empire of grocery stores, was a member of the conservative club but he had to be discreet about his allegiances because so many working-class voters who shopped at the branch of Everett's in St James Street voted Progressive. Quietly, he provided the Tories with committee rooms at elections and helped out the Primrose League. But not all shopkeepers and publicans were Elm House members: Herbert Antink, who owned an eel and pie shop on the High Street, was a Radical, as was George Crump, the landlord of the Flower Pot public house in Wood Street.

The Tories relied on a solid vote in the still largely rural areas of Chapel End, Higham Hill and Hale End, where the farmers and farmhands often voted the same way. John Hitchman, proprietor of the dairy Hitchman & Sons, owned Wadham Lodge Farm, Thorpe Hall Farm and rented Chestnuts Farm in Forest Road, and employed many farmhands and men and women to distribute the milk, which was organised from the main office at the corner of Church Hill and Hoe Street. Hitchman was elected for the Moderates in Wood Street ward after retiring. Radicals were naturally suspicious of the agricultural interest. A newspaper alleged that a farmer in Higham Hill escorted his labourers by horse and cart to a polling station to vote on election day.

Edward Good was another retired businessman turned Moderate politician after he had drifted away from Radicalism and embraced Conservative ideals. He had moved out of Gladstone Villa in Pembroke

Mary Auckland, a milkmaid working for J. Hitchman & Sons, with a dairy cart. (Courtesy of Vestry House Museum, London Borough of Waltham Forest)

Road after making a fortune and into Cleveland House from where he was elected for Hoe Street ward and later the Board of Guardians, and Essex County Council. He handed over Good Brothers to his sons, who opened a builders' merchants, and focused on good works and civic affairs. But not everyone was impressed with Good's foray into local politics. 'A very poor, halting and hesitating speaker,' was how the *Walthamstow Reporter* described him in action at the Town Hall.

By 1900 the Radical surge behind Woods was faltering. He had undermined his popularity with his muddled stance on the Boer War, voicing opposition at one point and then voting in Parliament for military supplies, or 'spewing Radical-cum-jingo cobblers on the war', as the branch newspaper of the SDF put it. In the summer of 1900, at the official opening of Lloyd Park, Woods was heckled by SDF supporters. At that year's general election, Woods was defeated and soon the Progressives lost their majority on the council. McSheedy's erratic behaviour partly contributed to their setback. He had libelled one Moderate rival and had a punch-up with another political opponent inside the Town Hall.

The Progressives were being challenged by the SDF in their strongholds. Alexander Bowman, an insurance salesman from Belfast, was one of fourteen party members who contested all four of Walthamstow's wards in the Essex County Council elections of 1894. They polled few votes and the next summer Bowman returned to Belfast. His departure delighted local Progressives who had accused the SDF of splitting the anti-Tory vote after the socialists started to contest St James ward, which they felt to be their fiefdom. A local newspaper sympathetic to the Progressives denounced Bowman as the leader of the socialist 'wreckers', who had an unholy alliance with the Tories. The SDF persisted. In 1900 George Hewitt ran in St James Street with the main plank in his platform of challenging landlordism. Out of spite copies of *Justice*, the party's paper, were withdrawn from the reading rooms at the public library.

SDF members later supported an independent Labour ticket in local elections and in 1906 a slate of candidates stood on a socialist-influenced programme, including advocating that the council build houses for people. Val McEntee stood in St James ward with the coal porter John Hayward, who was a Christian socialist, teetotaler and vegetarian, while Fred Krailing, a confectionery manager, and Fred Sturge ran in the High Street ward. They were all defeated. They had hoped for a breakthrough and had thrown resources into the election, organising a public meeting at the Public Baths addressed by Will Thorne, a Labour MP, and Henry Hyndman, the leader of the SDF. Undeterred, John Hayward and Helen Campbell stood the next year on the same Labour ticket for the Board of Guardians of the West Ham Poor Law Union.

Their activities were not limited to electioneering. Krailing and McEntee were superintendents at the Walthamstow Socialist Sunday School, which had its own ten commandments, the first one being 'Love your schoolfellows, they will become your fellow workers and companions in life'. The socialist message was spread with the help of a horse-drawn Clarion van, a mobile propaganda unit named after *The Clarion* newspaper, which pulled up at a street corner for activists to distribute leaflets and literature. There were plenty of rallies addressed by Pete Curran, a Labour MP for Jarrow who lived on the Warner's Clock House estate, at the Recreation Ground in Selbourne Road. A Labour activist called Mary Salt opened one demonstration at 'the Rec' by singing a chorus of the Victorian hymn 'God Save the People'. In 1905 Val McEntee led a deputation of the unemployed to a council meeting and spoke, warning the councillors about the hardship and misery of the many jobless men and women and their families. He condemned the Progressive majority for still intending to cut the rates and demanded public works to provide jobs as some of the unemployed whistled 'La Marseillaise' during the meeting.

Walthamstow's Labour candidates now had a high-profile supporter. Frances Greville, Countess of Warwick was a member of the Maynard family, owners of Walthamstow Toni manor, who had been born into a life of wealth and privilege. But Lady Warwick converted to socialism after meeting Robert Blatchford, editor of *The Clarion*, and by 1905 had joined the SDF and actively campaigned for Labour candidates, visiting Walthamstow many times. In 1905 she toured constituencies across the country in a motor car to rally support for Labour.

Yet most working people voted Progressive or Liberal. The Liberal and Radical Club at Grove House in Buxton Road had many members, including a railway porter named Walter Osbourne who was a staunch anti-socialist. Osbourne was secretary of the Walthamstow branch of the Amalgamated Society of Railway Servants but had been expelled for opposing the union's financial support for Labour Party candidates through a political levy. Osbourne started a legal challenge, fighting all the way to the House of Lords and winning a landmark ruling in 1909. To those who saw him as denying the wishes of union members he was a villain but to Liberals he was a hero and Osbourne, who had been a councillor, was given the honour in 1909 of opening the new public library in the High Street, next to the baths. He also helped unveil a Stars and Stripes and a Union flag from the bust of the philanthropist Andrew Carnegie set in a niche over the front door of the building.

Women were increasingly involved in local politics. Since 1894 women could vote in district council elections and they were beginning to stand for office in local government. In 1900, Mrs Makepeace and Mrs Ellison were elected to the School Board as two of the candidates for the Ratepayers' Association. But the biggest mobiliser of women from all backgrounds was the women's suffrage movement which campaigned for women to have the vote, and to be able to stand as candidates, at elections for Parliament. A branch of the Women's Social and Political Union (WSPU) was founded and in 1910 their supporters used another by-election in Walthamstow to maximise support for their cause.

The National Union of Women's Suffrage Societies opened committee rooms in Hoe Street and brought in activists to fight the Liberal candidate because the Asquith government had blocked legislation in Parliament to grant women the vote. National leaders of the women's suffrage campaign such as Christabel and Emmeline Pankhurst and Mrs Pethwick Lawrence appeared in Walthamstow. As voting day approached they organised a procession of hundreds of women starting near to their offices in Hoe Street, which marched to Walthamstow Palace. A suffragette who had been imprisoned fighting for the cause took part in the parade, which was led by a woman on horseback holding a white, purple and green flag, the colours of the women's suffrage movement.

Not everyone advocated change through the ballot box. Revolutionaries made a headline-grabbing appearance in 1909 when two men who had been members of a revolutionary organisation in Tsarist Russia robbed a factory in Tottenham and fled firing semi-automatic pistols, killing a policeman and a boy. They were pursued by the police across the marshes to Walthamstow, where they hijacked a tram and two carts before they were cornered at a cottage in Hale End. One was shot dead by the police and the other died of his injuries days later. The event became known as the Tottenham Outrage.

That year a journalist named Guy Bowman (he had no connection to the Irish SDF member) had rented a house in Maude Terrace on the Clock House estate. He was a syndicalist, believing that the trade unions should replace the state and take over the organisation of society through a general strike. Special Branch had a file on him because in 1906 he had been expelled from Spain after attempting to interview a man involved in a plot to assassinate the Spanish king. Bowman, as the Metropolitan Police

Commissioner noted, wasn't a man of action, he believed in spreading syndicalism by the written word.

By 1912 he was publisher of *The Syndicalist*, the newspaper of the Industrial League led by Tom Mann, which Bowman had arranged to be printed by Charles and Ben Buck at their printing shop at Stainforth Road in Walthamstow. As strikes shook the country, Bowman published an article in the newspaper written by Mann entitled 'Don't Shoot!' calling on soldiers to side with strikers. Special Branch raided the brothers' printing works, seizing letters to Bowman dating from 1911, account books, receipts and printer's proofs of *The Syndicalist Railwayman* and older editions of *The Syndicalist*, then searched Bowman's house. The three men were later charged under an obscure mutiny law.

At the trial the prosecution alleged that the men's actions were seditious and made great play of an advertisement which was printed in the same

The Daily Mirror

THE MORNING JOURNAL WITH THE SECOND LARGEST NET SALE.

No. 2,623. SATURDAY, MARCH 23, 1912 One Halfpenny.

PREACHERS OF SEDITION SENTENCED: PRISONERS IN THE "SYNDICALIST" CASE SENT TO HARD LABOUR AT THE OLD BAILEY.

The Syndicalist

Edited under the auspices of the Industrial Syndicalist Education League

Vol. 1. No. 2. FEBRUARY, 1912. MONTHLY, One Penny.

Now for the Fight. | A NATIONAL FEDERATION OF OUR TRADES COUNCILS.

THE SYNDICALIST

A Hopeful Start.

Enthusiastic Syndicalist Leaguers open the campaign of 1912, with a happy combination of frolic and zeal.

Open Letter to British Soldiers.

Sabotage.

Preachers of Sedition: the mutiny trial of the Buck brothers and Bowman. (Courtesy of Mirrorpix, The *Daily Mirror*, 1912) edition of *The Syndicalist* as the offending article promoting the King air rifle. Unfortunately for Bowman's defence, he had printed the advert with the caption: 'Learn to shoot straight: The air rifle will help every young and old syndicalist'. The Old Bailey jury took fifteen minutes to find them guilty; Bowman received nine months' hard labour and the brothers got six months, although the sentences were later cut following a campaign supported by a few MPs. On 23 March 1912 the front page of the *Daily Mirror* called them the 'Preachers of Sedition'.

The brothers, whose involvement with Bowman was more commercial than political, were well known in labour movement circles in Walthamstow and had supported the William Morris Hall in Somers Road, which opened in 1909 and was used for meetings by many branches of the trade unions active in the town.

Trade unions were increasing in strength, particularly among the low-skilled, and Walthamstow Trades Council was established as a coordinating body. From 1897 large numbers of workmen toiled at the Lockwood and Banbury Reservoirs for contractors working for the East London Water Company. They operated cranes and steam-powered diggers and laboured in butty gangs, working on a piece rate shared among the men, as they

A steam engine at work at the Lockwood and Banbury Reservoirs around 1900. (London Metropolitan Archives, courtesy of Thames Water)

shifted huge amounts of peat and earth to divert the old River Lea from its old course and build the Lockwood and Banbury Reservoirs, which they completed by 1903. The Walthamstow branch of the Navvies' Union was strong, and in the days before a welfare state the Navvies' Mission organised a Slate Club into which members paid 6*d* a week and could claim 10*s* a week for nine weeks as sick pay.

Building workers were increasingly unionised. A general building labourer named Eli Rose had his membership certificate of the General Labourers' Amalgamated Union proudly framed at his home in Hazelwood Road and attended open-air street meetings outside The Bell, called by the Building Trades Federation, representing all the building unions, to discuss grievances. The urban district council was a union stronghold. The Radicals had courted the union vote, and McSheedy, who regarded himself as a man of the people, addressed meetings of the municipal unions but, once in power, his Progressives came into conflict with the increasingly militant lamplighters and workers at the Low Hall sewage farm, who were unafraid to strike for higher pay.

The most downtrodden of Walthamstow's workers, although they had no trade union, were the young, female and poorly paid domestic servants. A new domestic servant was often recruited by a small advert. At Cedars Avenue a Mrs Allen advertised for a servant, stipulating 'good character indispensable; no washing; wages £12', while her neighbour Mrs Collier was searching for a 'thorough servant who could cook for £16'. Unsurprisingly, many young women chose the new factories which were starting to appear in Walthamstow over the badly paid and low-status life of domestic service, even working at Gillard's pickling plant at the Vintry Works off the High Street in which a largely female workforce toiled from 8 a.m. to 7 p.m. for little pay.

Trade unions were active in many of the engineering factories which were starting to concentrate around Blackhorse Lane by the turn of the century, and vehicle manufacturing was one of the main industries established in the area after Vanguard Omnibus Works shifted production to the area from London. Walthamstow had its own automotive pioneer Frederick Bremer. His four-cylinder motor car never went into mass production, but Bremer could be seen driving his prototype around with a man waving a red warning flag walking in front.

The writer Richard Fox later recalled the stress of working at a Blackhorse Lane factory, which had adopted scientific management techniques so that the foremen measured operatives' times for assembling engines by a stopwatch and made sure that every second of production time could be accounted for. There was an atmosphere of fear and mistrust, even among the workers. One young man walked home each night with his pockets crammed with bolts and nuts because he was afraid they would disappear during the night, and men hid tools to stop others getting to them. Fox joined the union, but when he told a workmate that he had gone to a political meeting instead of working overtime, the man looked with amazement that he had chosen to miss out on 'alf a sov'.

The Blackhorse Lane factories were one of the few expanding local sources of employment in what had become a dormitory town. Most breadwinners worked elsewhere, many of them in London, and had to endure the rush-hour commute and the daily slog of travelling in and out on crowded rail carriages. Many people's working lives were organised around the railway timetable. Rush hour was unpleasant and the trains overcrowded. London County Council investigators discovered in 1898 that on 18 April the last of the six trains from Walthamstow accepting workman's fares left St James Street at 6.12 a.m., and there was seating for 2,810 passengers but an estimated 4,030 people crammed on board. A porter prevented access to the first-class carriage.

Martha Pearson, a widow with three children who worked as a machinist, told Commissioners investigating railway services that she took the 5.55 a.m. train from St James Street but didn't start work until 9 a.m., which meant she was forced to kill time sitting in a waiting room at Liverpool Street. William Harthord, a cellarman at Crosse & Blackwell, told the same hearing that he had moved to Walthamstow because of the workman's fare, but had given up catching the early morning workmen's trains, opting to pay the higher 4*d* fare to avoid exhaustion and wasting so much spare time when he got into London.

By the late 1890s Great Eastern experimented with running trains through the night to Liverpool Street every half hour for night workers and those on early shifts. Morning and night people poured in and out of Hale End station as men and women, many of whom came up by train from Homerton, clocked on for shifts at the British Xyonlite Company, which opened a factory in 1897 on the site of an old farm, producing plastic combs, brushes and ping-pong balls. A sketch writer for the *Daily Chronicle*, who watched the exhausted clerks and operatives trudging out of the third-class exit at Hoe Street in the evening, described the growing town as 'one of the great dormitories of the metropolis … without much stretch of the imagination its houses are cubicles to which weary men retire at night after fighting the battle of life in the great city'. Yet when people returned in the evening they found there was plenty of life in the town.

The weary returning to Hoe Street station after a day's work. (The *Daily Chronicle*. Illustration by Charles Pears, Courtesy of the British Library and Solo Syndication)

In 1903 the Walthamstow Palace opened in the High Street with a first night slapstick show performed by Fred Karno's company. In the evenings it ran a full programme of variety, revues and band shows, bringing in artistes who performed across the London variety circuit. The Palace, owned by Syndicate Halls which had built variety venues across north London, was built to stand out on the High Street with polished red-brick and Bath stone topped by turrets and flagpoles. Inside, little expense had been spared on furnishing the theatre with gilt fittings, velvet hangings and a marble staircase leading up to the balconies. The Palace was incredibly popular when it opened. The only blemish was a wire mesh stretched across the balcony to stop those in the cheapest seats raining orange peel down on to people sitting in the stalls below.

Variety shows at the Palace competed with performances at other public entertainment venues such as the Victoria Hall in Hoe Street, which opened in 1887. There were also concerts and music recitals on a Sunday evening at the Public Baths, which had with rooms for public gatherings, and there were events at the Conway Hall opposite the Baths on the High Street.

Sundays were an important leisure day. The building labourer Eli Rose, who often worked more than fifty hours a week, would stroll with his family to the Recreation Ground, the 'Rec', in Selbourne Road for Band Sunday at 2 p.m., which often finished with a march of the competing brass bands around the town. He recorded in his diary for 1895 that on other Sundays he would often read *Lloyd's Weekly* in the morning at his home, usually taking a close interest in the latest ghoulish murder. In the afternoon he and his wife Caroline would 'put on our best cloth' and walk up to Walthamstow cemetery with their three children to pay their respects at the grave of their youngest son. Rose was a strong teetotaler and member of the Samson Lodge of the Sons of Phoenix and on other Sunday afternoons he would stroll up to an open-air meeting at Markhouse Common.

For self-improvers the urban district council's Technical Instruction Committee organised a series of lectures at Grosvenor House, which the district council had taken over, offering talks on subjects such as 'The Chemistry of Air, Fire and Water', and the School Board held evening classes in typewriting for adults.

In an era of rapid technological change, A.V. Roe famously flew his triplane on Walthamstow marshes in 1909, and with increasing urbanization (Walthamstow's population rose remorselessly from 96,720 in 1901 to reach 124,580 by 1911) there was a growing interest in the area's past and heritage. Hand-painted postcards started to appear of the old remaining lanes, the Ancient House, St Mary's Church, Monoux's almshouses and the Water House in Lloyd Park. Even some of Walthamstow's old weather-boarded cottages, which would have been considered hovels and an embarrassing relic of the rural past in the 1880s, found their way onto postcards. Schoolmaster George Bosworth started his 'Walthamstow of Yesterday' lectures at the public library, featuring lantern slides of the Wilcumestou folio in the Domesday Book, and charted Walthamstow's history back to an Anglo-Saxon past. Bosworth and others founded the Walthamstow Antiquarian Society in 1914.

Sports clubs were playing an increasingly important role in people's leisure time. Watching Walthamstow Town football team on a Saturday afternoon, thanks to half-day working introduced in factories and workshops, was popular and Walthamstow soon had its own amateur league of twenty football clubs. Cycling was booming. Many people, particularly increasing numbers of women, bought their first bicycle at Walthamstow's specialist bicycle shops or manufacturers such as Lane's on Queens Road or from George Fearn, who made wringers and mangles in St James Street and sold cycles to meet the demand. In the spring, cyclists could be seen spinning along Forest Road (as Clay Street and Hagger Lane had recently been renamed) and turning sections of the road into a racetrack. Pedestrians had to watch out!

Cinema was the biggest change to people's leisure time. In 1907, the Victoria Theatre became the Walthamstow Picture Theatre and the Prince's Pavilion in the High Street opened in 1909. Good Brothers were Walthamstow's own cinema pioneers. Edward Good's sons built cinemas and ran their builders' merchants. They opened the Queen's Cinema in 1911 behind their row of shops in Hoe Street with the entrance for customers through a house next door, the Arcadia at Wood Street in 1912 and Empire Cinema at the Bell Corner. Cinemas may even have shown films which were made in the area as a film production industry had been established on Hoe Street by the early twentieth century, and there was Broad West Film Studios operating in Wood Street. But it wasn't just cinemas which were opening on Walthamstow's main streets.

Walthamstow's shops were booming. Attractive new premises, which had glass facades, gilded window lettering and hanging signs, opened in parts of St James Street, High Street and Hoe Street, and even the Ancient House at Church End was converted into shops. A highlight of the civic year was the annual Cart Horse Parade in which a procession of nags, ponies and

Walter West looking into the camera at Broad West Film Studios in Wood Street in 1915. (Courtesy of Vestry House Museum, London Borough of Waltham Forest)

The Ancient House was converted into shops by the 1880s. (Courtesy of Vestry House Museum, London Borough of Waltham Forest

Walthamstow had many street entertainers including Blind Harry of Wood Street, pictured in 1917. (Courtesy of Vestry House Museum, London Borough of Waltham Forest)

horses pulled carts decorated with flags and bunting owned by tradesmen and shopkeepers around the town, and Lady Leucha Warner gave out the prizes one year.

In 1882, the Board of Health had changed the old historic name of Marsh Street to High Street after a petition by local shopkeepers who were eager it should become recognised as Walthamstow's main shopping area. The well-to-do viewed the market as another symptom of social decline of the area into something resembling the East End and were disturbed by the ponies, carts and barrows, and the traders selling late into Friday and Saturday night who left rotting rubbish. The High Street was also a place for popular musical entertainment such as barrel organ players. Sometimes large crowds gathered to listen to a steam organ or watch a circus performance in a field nearby.

Local tradesmen developed shops. A new row of shops called Ambrose Terrace was built in the 1890s by William Norwood, who had started in trade as a butcher and acquired enough capital to go into building. He also built part of Hatherley Mews behind the parade. He put up housing, including his own large house on Hatherley Terrace called Norwood House, which had a bust of himself over the main entrance and was around the corner from Norwood's butchers on Hoe Street, which delivered cuts of meat by cart to homes in the area.

The new shops in the St James Street district stirred civic pride. By 1900 Warner's Clock House estate, including a parade of shops, had been completed with up-to-date shops decorated with cornicing, pediments and window mullions, as well as terracotta ornaments of griffins and sea gods. In 1897, Reuben Jolly opened the jewel in his retail crown: Everett's model

Mr Eastwell delivered meat with his cart for a branch of Norwood's butchers in Hoe Street. (Courtesy of Vestry House Museum, London Borough of Waltham Forest)

St James Street in 1906 with one of the new trams rolling past a branch of Everett's. (Mary Evans Picture Library)

Barrett's greengrocer and fruiter in Hoe Street displaying its goods. (Courtesy of Vestry House Museum, London Borough of Waltham Forest)

bakery in St James Street. It had steam ovens, which were healthier than the old coal or wood-fired ovens still used by many bakers, and was powered by electricity. Jolly kept his prices low and advertised Everett's loaves to local shoppers as 'the most healthful, economical and never tiring food in the world'.

The competition was fierce and shop workers' hours behind the counter were very long. There had been attempts to have voluntary early closing of some grocer's, but the initiatives failed and it was only when Acts to regulate shop hours were introduced by Parliament that working hours for shop staff began to fall.

The street market, with costermongers' barrows and stalls, had grown up along St James Street and into the High Street, and now competed with the shopkeepers to supply foodstuffs to working people. As a result, there was increasing antagonism between the shopkeepers and the stall traders and costermongers, whom they regarded as pests, as Walthamstow's street market spread up from St James Street to the High Street. Many costermongers ignored regulations for setting out stalls and barrows and the authorities winked at the 'nuisance'. In 1901 stalls were removed and traders prosecuted, sparking accusations by some Radicals that the clampdown had been encouraged by shopkeepers at Elm House after the Moderates had retaken control of the council. Some traders took matters into their own hands. John Blackburn, a fruit seller of Buxton Road, took legal action after the stall he set up outside Lidstone's on the High Street was picked up by six employees of the drapers and dumped in the road, upsetting the trader's precious stock of fruit.

But there was one competitor the shopkeepers truly feared. The Co-operative Movement, which was renowned for good quality and reasonable prices, had been growing in Walthamstow since the first Co-operative Society was founded in 1886 and numbered 229 members by 1899. The first store was in Markhouse Road, and premises were later opened in Clarendon Road until the local society merged with the Stratford Co-operative and Industrial Society and in 1912 opened an enormous store on Hoe Street. The founders put up a plaque with a beehive, the co-operators' symbol, on the store.

Since the late nineteenth century a community of German shopkeepers, many of them butchers, had been established in Walthamstow but in the summer of 1914 they now discovered that they were regarded as the enemy within. As war loomed Philip Streitenberger, a butcher in the High Street, resorted to taking out adverts in a local newspaper declaring, 'I am a Britisher

The market stalls opening late on a Saturday night at the end Hoe Street near the Baker's Arms towards Leyton. (The *Daily Chronicle*. Illustration by Charles Pears, Courtesy of the British Library and Solo Syndication)

and not a German' and in September 1914 a large crowd gathered outside a butchers owned by Karl Hoffman in Wood Street demanding the owner remove a Union flag. Many young men enlisted in the Essex Regiment and other units to fight and there were patriotic demonstrations and rallies in support of the war efforts as there were in towns and cities all over the country. People were mobilising for a war in which even Walthamstow would be a target.

10

The People's Century

In 1919 Wallace Barltrop was demobbed from the Royal Air Force after serving as a motorcycle dispatch rider in France with 110 Squadron. He was one of around 22,000 local men who had served, including other members of the Barltrop family in Walthamstow. His brother Horace Barltrop fought as an infantryman in the Essex Regiment but he was killed in action in the Middle East aged just 22.

As families remembered their dead, funds were being raised in many churches, workplaces and schools for memorials to those who fought or died. The men at the Xylonite factory who served had a plaque unveiled in their honour, while employees of the Walthamstow tram system commemorated the eleven colleagues who were killed. Marsh Street Congregrational Church unveiled a plaque, as did Blackhorse Road School. A cenotaph memorial was erected in front of Lloyd Park in 1922 and a stone cross was put up in front of Walthamstow Lodge, Church Hill, used by the 7th Battalion, Essex Regiment as a headquarters and recruiting station during the war to remember those who had died.

Civilians had been caught up in the death and destruction. When Zeppelins raided London on the night of 17/18 August 1915 they had, after attacking factories in the Lea Valley, dropped an incendiary bomb first on Lloyd Park, then dropped more bombs on Hoe Street, Lea Bridge Road and streets in Leyton, killing ten people and injuring many more. In 1918 a Gotha plane

The aftermath of the bomb which fell behind the Rose and Crown in 1918. (Courtesy of Vestry House Museum, London Borough of Waltham Forest)

dropped a 100kg bomb which landed behind the Rose and Crown pub in Hoe Street, destroying many houses in Richards Place. Miraculously no one was killed.

Those on the home front worked around the clock. Arthur Newman, a clicker in the boot trade who lived on Chatham Road, worked for a manufacturer in Tottenham making boots for the army. He was exempted from conscription because of the need for skilled labour in 1916, but was called up in 1917 despite his employer's appeals. Women took over the jobs which had long been considered the preserve of men.

When peace returned, factories stepped up production and Walthamstow became more of a place of work than it had been in the nineteenth century. The Associated Equipment Company (AEC), which was formed out of the Vanguard Omnibus Company, started to manufacture the Reliance bus and by the 1920s the first trolleybuses, which would replace trams on the roads. Blackhorse Lane became a booming industrial area with engineering plants, delivery yards and factories, and Café Rodi on Blackhorse Lane opened in the 1920s to feed the hungry who worked in the factories or yards in the area. Every day thousands of men and women poured into the area to work in the factories.

Modernist buildings for engineering companies sprang up in the 1930s. Fullers Electric in Fulbourne Road won a contract from the Central

The unveiling of the cenotaph at the Water House on Forest Road. (Courtesy of Vestry House Museum, London Borough of Waltham Forest)

Electricity Board to build new grid transformers. Hammond & Champness opened the modernist Gnome House in Blackhorse Lane in 1930, making lifts. To help prepare young people for technical jobs in modern industry, the South West Essex Technical College and School of Art was opened in 1938. It was soon called the People's University. In the first academic year 6,842 students, mainly taking evening classes, enrolled, studying everything from engineering to architecture, commerce and languages. Grosvenor House and Chestnuts house in Hoe Street were used to meet the demand. Nearby Cleveland House had been taken over as a branch of Clarke's College in 1913 to teach shorthand, typewriting and office skills, and prepare youngsters for civil service exams.

Many workers in Walthamstow's new offices and factories were sympathetic to the Labour Party which, in 1919, had a breakthrough when it won four seats on the urban district council and in 1921 won a slim majority. Lady Warwick still supported the local party, attending events and opening bazaars. The old alignment of Progressives and Moderates disintegrated and was replaced by Labour, Liberal and Conservative candidates contesting each ward as representatives of national parties; only Hoe Street ward held out against the trend.

Labour set out to improve people's living conditions with zeal and for the first time the council started to build its own houses, which had long been the dream of Labour supporters in Walthamstow, thanks in part to new subsidies from central government. The largest estate at Higham Hill had 950 homes and new council housing was also built at Hale End. The Labour councillors also co-operated with the Warner estate company, which had bought up the land at Moons Farm to build a new estate off Billet Lane, close to its existing Winns estate. The old farm was knocked down for housing and Warner was unsympathetic to a member of Walthamstow Antiquarian Society who hoped to preserve the old barn. At the Public Baths in the High Street the famous slipper baths were opened in 1923, allowing many of the poorest residents to have regular baths during the week.

The worst of the nineteenth-century housing was demolished between the wars. At Wood Street, Jeffries Square came down in 1933 and the elderly residents who were the remnants of a once tight-knit community had to leave. They included the house painter Edward Timms, who had lived around Wood Street since the 1880s. Cottages in a yard behind the Carlton Cinema came down in 1933, followed by the slum of Markhouse Place. The borough's population was still rising: by the 1931 census the population had hit a peak of 132,972 people, creating an even greater demand for housing.

Walthamstow was regarded as a radical local authority. In 1926, during the General Strike, the municipal leaders even agreed to turn off the current generated by the electricity power station after its workers threated to strike, but the district council was fined after complaints by local manufacturers. The area's radical reputation delayed Walthamstow's application to become a borough, which was supported by all parties including the Moderates, but not for long.

In 1929 Walthamstow celebrated becoming a municipal borough, which had significantly greater powers than the urban district council. A public commemoration took place with military bands in September 1929, at which the Royal Charter of Incorporation was officially presented to the Charter Mayor of Walthamstow, Sir Theydon Courtenay Warner, by the top-hatted and frock-coated Lord Privy Seal Jimmy Thomas, a former trade unionist and Labour MP. But that wasn't the celebration which most people remembered in the town.

Walthamstow celebrated becoming a borough with a historical pageant acted by schoolchildren in 1930. The idea came from Constance Demain Saunders, and was supported and written by other members of Walthamstow Antiquarian Society, in particular the borough librarian George Roebuck and George Bosworth. In twelve episodes it set out Walthamstow's history, starting with Wilcumestou and Ralph de Toni, through to John Ball and the Peasants' Revolt, George Monoux, Disraeli and William Morris in the nineteenth century. In the epilogue, all the historical characters appear for the final scene along with the new borough's coat of arms with the William Morris-inspired legend: Fellowship is Life.

The pageant was performed at the Palace for three nights in October 1930, with 600 children on stage, and schoolchildren attending each performance. It was judged to have been an outstanding success; the children's acting and costumes were particularly commended and it was repeated in 1934 for the centenary of William Morris's birth. One of the best scenes according to the local newspapers was the appearance in Wilcumestou of John Ball, a completely fictitious historical event made up for the pageant, who gives a rousing speech to the people, inspiring them to march on London and join the Peasants' Revolt.

The pageant was one of the ways of instilling civic pride and an understanding of Walthamstow's history among a younger generation. Constance Demain Saunders had also presented a series of illuminated pictures telling Walthamstow's story to the central library, where they are on display today. She also gave Vestry House, where she had lived after it had been converted for domestic use, for use as the borough's local history museum, which opened in 1932. The curator Annie Hatley gathered hundreds of objects donated by local people, including the prototype of Frederick Bremer's four-cylinder car, while the borough's librarian George Roebuck lobbied the British consul in Rome for the return of a ninth-century sword kept in a private collection, which he believed had been uncovered along with the Viking ship at the reservoirs in 1900.

Yet Walthamstow was losing the remnants of its rural past. Arable land just off Chingford Road was built on for the new Monoux school, which opened in 1927, and that year the building of the North Circular Road started, slicing through the grounds of Salisbury Hall Farm and Wadham Lodge Farm, and into the edge of the forest. The common marsh had probably not been used for grazing livestock since before the Great War, but in 1934 the old Lammas grazing rights of livestock were extinguished over 99 acres of remaining meadow and the borough was allowed to develop the area as a recreation ground.

In the 1930s greyhound racing started in what had been a rural area until the war. The first greyhound race took place in 1931 on a track and site with corrugated iron sheds, just across the road from the old Salisbury Hall farmhouse off Chingford Road. In 1933 the art deco Walthamstow Stadium, developed by William Chandler, was officially opened by the aviatrix Amy

Johnson. Race meetings at the 'Goodwood of greyhounds' were wildly popular, partly because betting was allowed in the stadium, with attendances of 15,000 or more people watching the dogs and enjoying a flutter. The Chandler family also promoted boxing and speedway at the iconic stadium, which quickly became a famous venue across Britain and a source of local pride. In 1934 the speedway team Walthamstow Wolves led by captain Dicky Case raced for a season in the London league.

It wasn't the only entertainment. There was a rebuilding of the Edwardian cinemas as film grew in popularity. Good Brothers increased seating at the Queen's to 800 to meet demand and by 1930 the Victoria Hall on Hoe Street was demolished and replaced by the Granada, which seated 2,697 and dazzled with a white stucco façade and a lavishly decorated Moorish interior by a Russian stage designer. Sadly, Walthamstow's film industry declined between the wars. The pre-war studios based in Wood Street had struggled to compete against the appeal of Hollywood films and the studios shut in 1932. Not even a version of *Dick Turpin* filmed in Epping Forest saved them.

Sunday film showings were unpopular with many who still regarded the Sabbath as a day for rest and worship and a referendum was organised in 1932 to give Walthamstow's people their say on the issue. Churches and chapels led the 'Keep Your Sunday' campaign, which was headed by the Reverend Oakley, Vicar of Walthamstow, while cinema owners organised the

Walthamstow Stadium's greyhound meeting attracted thousands. (Courtesy of Vestry House Museum, London Borough of Waltham Forest)

'Vote for Sunday Cinemas' movement. Local newspapers and trade unionists were split on the issue but the two MPs were for Sunday opening. During the referendum, banners appeared on cinemas and chapels for and against the proposal to allow Sunday film showings. In the end, 18,722 voted for Sunday opening and 9,584 against.

Those in work enjoyed rising living standards and could afford to spend more money on entertainment, but there were many in Walthamstow who experienced long periods of unemployment between the wars, particularly in the 1930s. Members of the Unemployed Workers' Movement disrupted council meetings demanding that the corporation provide public works and other support, and a Walthamstow Fellowship was set up to alleviate hardship for the unemployed. The Greek Theatre at Walthamstow School for Girls, which was a county council school from 1913, was built by unemployed men as part of a public works scheme organised by the West Ham Union and was opened in 1925 by the actress Sybil Thorndike with a performance of *Medea* at the outdoor theatre. The unemployed men also built the Greek porch at the theatre but stopped work for a week or so in 1926 to support the General Strike.

Political parties competed for the votes of the unemployed. Generally, Walthamstow retained its traditional political loyalties: Walthamstow East was solidly Conservative, apart from the odd general election, while Labour-leaning Walthamstow West elected Val McEntee in 1922 and Labour candidates consistently at every election between the wars. The Liberals were also still a force. But the British Union of Fascists and the Communist Party of Great Britain were also growing. Oswald Mosley spoke in Exmouth Road, guarded by Blackshirts. Walthamstow had a shul in Boundary Road and a synagogue in Queens Road, and the Jewish community, which had grown strongly during the early twentieth century, felt menaced. After one Fascist gathering, the windows of some Jewish-owned shops in Hoe Street were smashed.

The foreboding was correct. In 1939, Great Britain was at war again. This time people knew Walthamstow's factories would be top of the Luftwaffe target list. Civilians and children were evacuated and schools relocated to the Home Counties. The children of Markhouse Road School ended up in the village of Eaton Socon, Bedfordshire, where the teachers were given a large empty house as a school and used the greenhouse for biology lessons. Young men were called up to the Armed Forces as many of their fathers had been.

Walthamstow's people bravely endured the aerial war, living with rocket attacks, high-explosive bombs, sleeping in shelters and through black outs and rationing. Many also lived with the daily worry of loved ones serving in the Armed Forces. But civil defence was well organised with air-raid wardens, first aid, and teams to lead debris clearance, evacuation and providing supplies of food. Factories had prepared. Fullers Electric had gas detection and evacuation officers, and a gas-proof shelter for 660 people as well as first aid posts. Plants were converted to war production. The furniture makers F. Wrighton & Sons made parts for the wooden-framed Mosquito planes at their factory in Billet Lane.

The worst destruction was seen in 1944 as V1 and V2 rockets hit the borough. At Blackhorse Lane a rocket killed seventeen in a factory; another struck a shelter in Chingford Road, killing eight. The distribution centre for Hitchman's dairies off Hoe Street was destroyed, killing nineteen people and burying others in the debris. The western wing of the old Monoux almshouses was destroyed by a bomb in 1940.

As the people celebrated VE-Day in 1945 they were counting the high costs of war. Altogether, 71,849 properties had been damaged, 10,362 people had to be rehoused and 3,134 civilians had been killed. Many servicemen were also killed and new names were added to the Cenotaph and memorial cross at Church Hill.

But there were hopes for a better post-war world. At the general election, Val McEntee was returned for Walthamstow West and in Walthamstow East Harry Wallace grabbed the seat for the Labour Party on a swing of almost 15 per cent. The harbinger of change had come a few days before when Prime Minister Winston Churchill's rally at the Walthamstow Stadium flopped and his speech was drowned out in a tumult of booing and heckling, forcing him to abandon his appearance.

The borough set about addressing its housing needs. Prefab homes were erected and a permanent housing project called Priory Court Estate opened in 1947. The new housing, Walthamstow's first high-rise buildings, had 340 two-bedroom flats and sixty one-bedroom flats, which accommodated 1,600 people. Borough architect F.G. Southgate designed the blocks in a style influenced by *Zeilenbau* architecture, or 'building in a line', first pioneered in central Europe. Flats in the high-rise blocks, built of reinforced concrete on an east-west axis to catch the sunlight, had the luxury of radiators, stoves, service hatches, fridge, hot water, electricity and gas. Inside, the walls were decorated in blue and white cement paint with handrails painted in orange, all in a modernist design. Priory Court was a different world to the overcrowded Victorian terraced brick housing, which many of the new tenants had rented or lived in before the war. Priory Court was part of Southgate's vision for a modern Walthamstow. In 1946, the Reconstruction and Housing Committee published *Towards a Plan for Walthamstow*, which

VE-Day celebrations at Berwick Road in Walthamstow. (Courtesy of Vestry House Museum, London Borough of Waltham Forest)

was inspired by town planning ideas. In a few years, other new buildings appeared designed by Southgate. New flats were built on Hoe Street in the 1950s and Central Parade, with its striking modernist design and clock tower emblazoned with the borough coat of arms, was built in 1958.

Despite the rationing and shortages there was greater provision of public services. Prime Minister Clement Attlee, who was elected MP for Walthamstow West in 1950 after Val McEntee was ennobled to the House of Lords as Baron McEntee of Walthamstow, embodied this new ethos and was a great supporter of the borough's new public services. The borough was proud of its nursery school clinics, meals on wheels, pensioners' clubs and health centres. Heating was installed in the Public Baths, which opened all year round. In 1948, the Connaught Hospital in Orford Road joined the NHS. Attlee opened the William Morris Gallery in 1950.

Walthamstow's cultural progress was celebrated at the Festival of Britain in 1951, which included the beating of the bounds ceremony led by the chairman of the Walthamstow Antiquarian Society, Annie Hatley, and attended by children from several schools. There was also ballet, music, theatre and sports over the summer.

Industry sputtered back into life. While still a dormitory borough, there were about 40,000 people working in local industry including engineering, clothing and plastic goods by the 1950s. Walthamstow's toy industry took off. Britains at Sutherland Road in Higham Hill was one of the most successful

Priory Court was the flagship housing development in post-war Walthamstow. (Courtesy of Vestry House Museum, London Borough of Waltham Forest)

of Walthamstow's post-war companies, exporting toy farms and lead soldiers all over the world. Britains employed many, including female home-workers who sat at their kitchen tables hand-painting the toy soldiers until late into the night.

In the 1970s, factories began to shut as Walthamstow experienced industrial decline. The old Walthamstow Brewery in St James Street closed in that decade, as did the Halex factory in Highams Park and numerous other factories. Economic strife affected the workplace with an increase in strikes. In 1983 there was a strike at Britains over working hours when 200 workers walked out. It had moved to Blackhorse Lane from Sutherland Road in 1968.

In many workplaces trade unions were at the height of their power. At Fullers Electric shop stewards and management discussed everything at the joint consultation committee from heating in the canteen to the annual fortnight's holiday; in 1957 the workers voted for two weeks' leave in August. People worked and socialised together at Fullers, where the employees' sports and social club organised cricket matches, chess and judo clubs. Many of the factory's workers experienced their first taste of travel abroad on a club trip to Paris.

The rising affluence of many workers thanks to well-paid jobs at Fullers Electric and other modern plants meant people had more money to spend.

Shops in post-war Walthamstow started supplying fridges, televisions and other consumer goods as families started to spend greater leisure time in their more comfortable homes. But home entertainment meant the end for the variety theatres and Walthamstow Palace was knocked down in 1960, to be replaced with a shopping parade, and even the old cinemas started to struggle. The cinema at Bell Corner had become the Tatler Film Club by 1970.

As rationing came to an end, there was a greater variety of food to eat, and the first supermarkets opened in the 1960s. The street market in St James Street and the High Street remained popular, with stalls often owned by the same family, and today it is still going strong. In 1987, the indoor Heron Walk Shopping Centre, now called The Mall, was built. Sadly, the old Monoux school was demolished to make way for it.

Walthamstow lost many old buildings. In 1956, Grosvenor House was pulled down after a fire, followed by Northcott House in the High Street in 1964. Another house in the High Street called Chestnuts, behind which had been Gillard's pickling factory, was also lost, as were the Public Baths in 1968. Few of the old weather-boarded houses have survived, except for one or two around Wood Street. But there was a renewed interest in heritage. In 1967, Waltham Forest Council, into which the boroughs of Walthamstow, Leyton and Chingford had been amalgamated in 1965, designated Church End as a conservation area, which is the area today known as Walthamstow Village. Enthusiasts also protected the local heritage. The old Marshall steam engines were left at the pump house near Low Hall Lane when it became redundant in the 1970s and were preserved. The Pump House Museum later opened and the old Marshall steam engines first installed in 1896 are still operated today for visitors.

Post-war Walthamstow saw a blossoming youth culture. Young people had more money than ever in the 1950s and '60s thanks to full employment. Many started apprenticeships. Britains offered a three-year apprenticeship in the painting department and Fullers apprenticeships were highly sought after. The boys often began aged 15 and had to apply for a deferment from National Service. That didn't mean they escaped wearing a uniform because the company's regulation boiler suits had to be worn at all times.

Live music was incredibly popular. The Granada Cinema was re-launched as a major music venue and in 1958 Buddy Holly played there, followed in 1961 by John Coltrane and Dizzy Gillespie. When the Beatles supported Roy Orbison in the 1960s, 4,000 youngsters queued down Hoe Street to get in. The Assembly Hall at the Town Hall, which opened in 1943, was also a live music venue. There were also plenty of record shops. The most famous of them was Small Wonder Records on Hoe Street from 1975 to 1983, stocking heavy metal, progressive rock and punk, and running a record label. Nightclubs opened, including Charlie Chan's at Walthamstow Stadium in 1984. Pop music catapulted Walthamstow into the nation's consciousness with the success of the band East 17, who named their debut album *Walthamstow* in honour of their area.

Young people also had interests beyond pop culture. There was a desire to get outdoors and youth movements such as the Scouts and Girl Guides were strong and the Robin Hood Fellowship of the Woodcraft Folk met in the Co-op hall in Hoe Street. Perhaps the biggest rite of passage for children was learning to ride a bike and passing the National Proficiency Standard in cycling. For older adolescents there was the thrill of riding a motorbike or learning to drive and from the 1960s the streets filled up with motorcars, causing roads to be widened. Not even the opening of the Victoria Line extension to Walthamstow in 1968 halted the remorseless rise of congestion and traffic snarl-ups.

Walthamstow was losing population rapidly in the post-war world. The number of people living there fell to 121,135 by 1950 and at least 1,325 had chosen to leave and start life afresh in the Essex new towns. In 1961, the population was 108,845, but there was an increasing number who had been born in the new Commonwealth countries who had started to settle since the 1940s. In the 1960s more people arrived in Walthamstow who had been born in India, Pakistan, Jamaica and other Caribbean countries. Many came to work in local factories or public services. A mosque was set up in a house in 1968 at Verulam Avenue, and a permanent mosque later opened in Queens Road. In the 1990s a new mosque was built in East Avenue.

The recently arrived communities often felt the brunt of discontent and anger stemming from the industrial decline of the 1970s as well as discrimination. The far right revived and there were far right meetings in the area in the 1970s. But many opposed them and there was strong opposition to racism led by an alliance of groups, includling Rock against Racism, which was set up in 1976, and active locally, holding a Carnival for Racial Harmony in 1978 at Selbourne Park Recreation Ground. Sadly, the graffiti and violent racist attacks did not completely stop.

In the 1980s there was a further loss of population. Poverty increased as joblessness and insecure employment grew. More factories were shut as the optimism of the immediate post-war years faded. The Priory Court estate, which had been a flagship housing project, experienced problems in the 1980s and was regenerated in the late 1990s. Walthamstow Stadium was

Walthamstow Market in the early 1980s as the population was becoming more diverse. (Courtesy of Vestry House Museum, London Borough of Waltham Forest)

also in decline and the last race at the greyhound track was held in 2008; in 2013 it was torn down, but the front facade remains. The loss of this iconic building, which was nationally famous, was a blow to civic pride.

Today Walthamstow's population is increasing again. It's a growing multi-cultural community made up of people from many different backgrounds and faiths who speak many different languages. Yet, migration to Walthamstow hasn't just been a recent phenomenon as its history shows. The dormitory town of the nineteenth century, which grew so rapidly in population, was largely made up of people who had relocated to Walthamstow from other parts of London, particularly the East End. In the early nineteenth century, people started to arrive from Essex and further afield. And we can go even further back to the medieval records, which show there were labourers born outside England here in the 1440s.

Walthamstow has been a settled area for centuries, perhaps continuously for many hundreds of years as new archaeological discoveries are suggesting. Walthamstow's history starts with those people settling in the area in the distant past and continues to today with those who have chosen to call it their home.

Bibliography and Sources

Introduction

1951 ceremony in Annie Hatley (ed.), *Across the Years: Walthamstow Memories* (Walthamstow, 1953); *Walthamstow Guardian*, 8 June 1951; *Walthamstow Post*, 31 May, 7 June 1951; Lammas Lands File L35.3 WFALSL

1 Man and Mammoth: From the Ice Age to the Romans

Henry Woodward, 'The Ancient Fauna of Essex', in *Transactions of the Essex Field Club*, Vol. 3 (1883) pp.3–8; Henry Woodward 'Prehistoric Man and the Animals Which he Hunted', pp.105–7, in Edward Buxton, *Epping Forest* (London, 1923) *The Leisure Hour*, 6 November 1869 and British Museum's online catalogue. Pile dwellings, see Annie Hatley, *Early Days in the Walthamstow District* (Walthamstow Antiquarian Society, 1933), pp.4–18; Robert Munro, *The Lake Dwellings of Europe* (London, 1890), pp.450–60; Colwyn Vulliamy, *The Archaeology of Middlesex and London* (London, 1930), p.251

Vinegar Alley site: *The Village* (spring 2017). Rhona Huggins, 'London and the River Lea' in *London Archaeologist*, Vol. 8–9 (1998), p.242

Black Path: A.D. Law, *The Streets of Waltham Forest Volume One* (London, 1974), p.14 also www.walthamforestwalks.info.

Iron Age agriculture: William Addison, 'The Making of the Essex Landscape', in *An Essex Tribute: Essays Presented to Frederick G. Emmison* , ed. K. Neale (London, 1987), p.47; C.S. and C.S. Orwin, *The Open Fields* (Oxford, 1967), pp.21–31; Fishing see 'Ferry Lane Industrial Estate: An Archaeological Evaluation' (Pre-Construct Archaeology, 2016), pp.24–28

Roman finds: British Museum online catalogue, W.R. Powell (ed.), *A History of the County of Essex* Vol. 3: *Roman Essex* (London, 1963), p.198, Roads in *Map of Roman Britain* (Ordnance Survey, 1928), pp.6–7; Miller Christy, 'On Roman

Routes in Essex', in *Transactions of the Essex Archaeological Society*, Vol. 8 (1923), pp.233–4. Roman settlements: Rhona Huggins, 'Excavation of a Late Roman Site at Sewardstone Hamlet, Waltham Holy Cross Essex 1968–75', in *Essex Archaeology and History*, Vol. 10 (1978), pp.185–6; Ebenezer Clarke, *A History of Walthamstow* (Walthamstow, 1861), p.7

2 Wilcume's Place: Anglo-Saxon Walthamstow

Anglo-Saxons: Elizabeth Ogborne, *The History of Essex* (London, 1814), pp.4–6; J.N.L. Myres, *The English Settlements* (London, 1937), pp.114–119; British Museum online catalogue; Melvyn Bragg, *The Adventure of English* (London, 2011), pp.6–9

Place names at P.H. Reaney, *The Place Names of Walthamstow* (Walthamstow Antiquarian Society, 1930), p. 38; P.H. Reaney, *The Place Names of Essex* (London, 1935), pp.103–5; Eilert Ekwall, *The Concise Dictionary of English Place-Names* (Oxford, 1960), pp.238–478; William George Searle, *Onomasticon Anglo-Saxonicum* (Cambridge, 1897), p.496; F.M. Stenton, 'The Historical Bearing of Place-Name Studies: The Place of Women in Anglo-Saxon Society', *Transactions of the Royal Historical Society*, Vol. 25 (1943), pp.6–13; Brynmor Morris, 'Old English Place Names' in *Sense of Place in Anglo-Saxon England*, ed. Richard Jones and Sarah Semple (Barnsley, 2013), p.55; ERO T/P 75/1. Settlement: John Blair, 'Exploring Anglo-Saxon Settlement', *Current Archaeology*, 5 June 2015

Dugout boat in *The Reliquary and Illustrated Archaeologist*, Vol. 12 (London, 1901), pp.54–5; Roy Switsur, 'Early English Boats', *Radio Carbon*, Vol. 31 No. 3 (1989), pp.1011–15; *The Essex Naturalist*, Vol. 12 (1901), pp.11–13; Sean McGrail, *Logboats of England and Wales Part 1* (Oxford, 1978), pp.28–30. For the supposed Viking ship, see *The Daily Graphic*, 9 July 1901: *Essex Naturalist*, Vol. 12 (Essex Field Club, 1901), pp.150–2; Valerie Fenwick, 'Was There a Body Beneath the Walthamstow Boat?' in *International Journal of Nautical Archaeology and Underwater Exploration*, Vol. 7 No. 3 (1978), pp.191–4

Scramasax: Joseph Bosworth and T. Northcote Toller (ed.), *An Anglo-Saxon Dictionary*, pp.853–4. For Danelaw boundary see Ann Williams, 'The Vikings in Essex, 871–917', in *Essex Archaeology and History*, 27 (1996), pp.92–101

Lammas rights: LMA ACC/2558/MW/SU/01/034/1724; Bosworth, Northcote Toller, *An Anglo-Saxon Dictionary*, p.540; Bourne at ERO T/M 324/1; Joseph Bosworth and T. Northcote Toller, *An Anglo-Saxon Dictionary*, p.136; Woodford Charter, *LangScape: The Language of Landscape: Reading the Anglo-Saxon Countryside*, http://langscape.org.uk, version 0.9, accessed 1 November, 2016. Moots at Miller Christy, 'The Essex Hundred-Moots: An Attempt to Identify their Meeting-Places', *Transactions of the Essex Archaeological Society*, Vol. 28 (1928), pp.193–4

3 *Villeins* and Villages: Life in the Medieval Manors

T.C. Chisenhale-Marsh, *Domesday Book Relating to Essex* (Chelmsford, 1864) p.156, p.183; *Bordars:* W. Raymond Powell, *Essex in Domesday Book* (Chelmsford, 1990), pp.3–5. Waltheof at Ogbourne, p.87; F.W. Maitland, *Domesday Book and Beyond* (Cambridge, 1907), pp.26–118; www.domesdaybook.co.uk. Assarting: William Richard Fisher, *The Forest of Essex* (London, 1887), pp.312–3; H.A. Doubleday (ed.), *The Victoria County History of Essex*, Vol. 1, pp.335–3

Manorial church: Daniel Lysons, *The Environs of London* (London, 1796), pp.205–19; P.H. Reaney (edited by A.D. Law), *The Church of St Mary, Walthamstow* (Walthamstow Antiquarian Society, 1969), pp.8–9; George Bosworth, *The Parish Church of Walthamstow* (1938), pp.7–8; St Mary's Building File W83.1 WFALSL

All wills are in George Fry, *Walthamstow Wills 1335–1559* (Walthamstow Antiquarian Society, 1921), pp.1–37; Bosworth, *St Mary's* (1938), pp.11–12; Tirwhit, Lysons *The Environs*, pp.210–11; Inscriptions at Strype, Survey of London (1720), [online] (hriOnline, Sheffield). Accessed 10.08.2017

Lanes: Reaney, *Place Names*, pp.34–38; ERO D/DFC 185. Markets at R.H. Britnell, 'Essex Markets Before 1350', in *Essex Archaeology and History*, Vol. 13, (1981), pp.15–16

King John: Thomas Duffy Hardy, *A Description of the Patent Rolls in the Tower of London*. Hugh Large trial: F.W. Maitland, *Select Pleas of the Crown Volume 1: 1200–1225* (London, 1888), pp.121–3. Salesbury trial: *Calendar of Patent Rolls 1381–1385* (London, 1897), pp.30–1

Manor names: Lysons, *The Environs*, pp.205–10; Ian Blair, 'A Moated Manor at Low Hall, Walthamstow' in *Essex Archaeology and History*, 33 (2002), pp.195–200

Walthamstow Toni *computus* ERO D/DU 36/14. Poll tax: Carolyn C Fenwick, *The Poll Taxes of 1377, 1379, and 1381, Part 1*, pp.173–86. Names: David Hey (ed.), *The Oxford Companion to Family and Local History* (Oxford, 2010), p.300

Le Braches: ERO D/DXj 14; John Field, *English Field Names*, p.267, Hale End, Reaney, Place-Names, pp.24–5, Alexander Forbes's 1699 Map. Meadows colonisation: Blair, 'A Moated Manor', p.192

Manorial information: P.H. Reaney, *The Court Rolls of The Rectory Manor Walthamstow* (Walthamstow Antiquarian Society, 1939), pp.6–11; P.H. Reaney, *The Court Rolls of Salisbury Hall* (Walthamstow Antiquarian Society, 1938), pp.8–15

Foreign labourers: England's Immigrants 1330–1550 (www.englandsimmigrants.com, version 1.0, 22 September 2017), www.englandsimmigrants.com/

Medieval debtors: TNA C 241/150/69; C 131/28/10

Clerk's land: R.E.G. Kirk (ed.), *Feet of Fines for Essex*, Vol. 3 (Colchester, Essex Archaeological Society), pp.86–253

Land market: Mark Fitch and Frederick Emmison (eds), *Feet of Fines for Essex*, Vol. 5, p.84; R.E.G. Kirk (ed.), *Feet of Fines for Essex*, Vol. 1, p.152.

4 Almshouses, Alehouses and Religion in a Tudor Town

Monoux and St Mary's: John Strype, *Memorials of Thomas Cranmer* (Oxford, 1840), p.70; Henry Fox-Bourne, *English Merchants* (London, 1866), p.160; *An Account of the Benefactions*, in *Rules and Orders Established for the Relief and Government of the Poor of the Parish of Walthamstow (1780)*, pp.27–8; Lysons, *The Environs*, p.213, Ogborne, p.83

Hogeson: Arthur Leach, *English Schools at the Reformation 1546–8* (London, 1898), p.75; Colby, *An Account*, p.30. Gascoigne: Ogborne, pp.93–94. Almshouse rules, James Gibson, *The Walthamstow Charities: Caring for the Poor 1500–2000* (Chichester, 2000), pp.6–8

Charity: *An Account*, p.30; F.G. Emmison, *Elizabethan Wills of South-West Essex* (Chelmsford, 1976), pp.17–60. Monoux causeway, Strype, *Memorials*, p.70; ERO Q/SR 198/139. Withipol: Lysons p.230. Population: Leach, p.75

Ancient House: Marjorie Batsford, *Timber-Framed Buildings in Waltham Forest* (Walthamstow Historical Society, 1980), pp.3–6; *Vestiges*, 9, August–September 1956); Articles in Ancient House Buildings File, WFALSL; Martin Bridge, *Tree-Ring Analysis of Timbers from the Ancient House* (London, 2001)

Ale houses: F.G. Emmison, *Elizabethan Life: Disorder* (Chelmsford, 1970), pp.202–19; Peter Clark, *The English Alehouse: A Social History 1200–1830* (London, 1983), pp.66–8. Women ale brewers: P.H. Reaney, *The Court Rolls of Salisbury Hall*, pp.8–18; ERO Q/SR 73/7-29, Q/SR 112/9-9A

Arthur Clifford (ed.), *The State Papers and Letters of Sir Ralph Sadler*, Vol. 2 (Edinburgh, 1809), pp.22–3. Moons farm: ERO D/DFC 185; Strype; Statute of Artificers ERO Q/SR 48/88. Priory, Reaney, *Rectory Manor*, p.15

Religion: Bosworth, *A History of St Mary's*, pp.6–12; John Foxe, *The Unabridged Acts and Monuments Online* or *TAMO* (1583 edition), Book 12, p.2127 (HRI Online Publications, Sheffield, 2011). Available from: www.johnfoxe.org [Accessed: 10.06.17]

Hale family: ERO Q/SR 78/46, T/A 418/53/61, T/A 418/60/32, Q/SR 96/47, T/A 418/60/34: Christopher Marsh, *Music and Society in Early Modern England* (Cambridge, 2013), p.261; Hale family Biography File WFALSL

5 Merchants, Mansions and Poachers: Walthamstow in the Seventeenth Century

Merchants: Untitled notes, Conyers Biography File 2 WFALSL; Corby, *An Account*, pp.32–4; Coward: H.D. Budden, *The Story of Marsh Street Congregational Church Walthamstow*, p.13: John Handby Thompson, 'A Note on William Coward', in *The Journal of the United Reformed Church History Society*, Vol. 7 (2005), pp.421–426. Marriage registers are in ERO WF/W83/1, Charles Maynard in *Morant's History of Essex*, Vol. 1 (1768), p.34

John Wood: Lysons p. 221 and ERO Q/SR 343/61; untitled note Merry Biography File WFALSL, yeoman Q/SBa 2/78

Mill: LMA ACC/2558/EL/A/33/016; K.R. Fairclough, 'Mills and Ferries along the Lower Lea', *Essex Archaeology and History*, 23 (1992), p.61; A.D. Law, *References to the Coppermill 1647–1839*, Copper Mill Buildings File W26.4 WFALSL

Brickmaking: Alexander Forbes 1699 map. Hearth tax and 'Essex Hearth Tax Returns Michaelmas 1670', Hearth Tax Online, Centre for Hearth Tax Research; 'Strype; Daniel Defoe, *A Tour through the Whole Island of Great Britain* (Dent, London 1962), pp.5–7; Bernard will TNA PROB 11/372/198

Roads: ERO Q/SR 253/52-54, Q/SR 294/33

Pepys' diary at www.pepysdiary.com 13 September 1667; 20 February, 1 August 1661, 11 September 1665, 17 July 1667, 5 July, 1 August 1667

George Bosworth: *The Rectory Manor Walthamstow* (Walthamstow Antiquarian Society, 1917), p.10

Forest: William Richard Fisher, *The Forest of Essex*, pp.210–221, Swainmote TNA C99/144; Poaching: ERO Q/SR 352/40, Q/SR 318/27; Q/SR 319/27, Q/SR 318/28; Holcroft D/DCv 2/4; ERO D/DCv 3/10; Commons: Clarke's, *The History*, pp.12–14; Trunkett will TNA PROB 11/348/538

6 Chartists, Paupers and Apprentices: Walthamstow in the Industrial Revolution

Workhouse: Stephen J. Barns, *Walthamstow Vestry Minutes: Churchwardens' and Overseers' Accounts 1710–1740* (Walthamstow Antiquarian Society, 1925), pp.14–20; Stephen J. Barns, *Walthamstow Vestry Minutes: Churchwardens' and Overseers' Accounts 1741–1771* (Walthamstow Antiquarian Society, 1926), pp.27–30; *Rules for the Government of the Poor in the Workhouse of the Parish of Walthamstow* (1780), pp.12–19; Stephen J. Barns, *Walthamstow Vestry Minutes: Churchwardens' and Overseers' Accounts 1772–1794* (Walthamstow Antiquarian Society, 1927); Minutes of the West Ham Union Poor Law Guardians 1837–41, Newham Archives and Local Studies Library

Charity: Clarke, *The History*, pp.21–62; William Wilson, *Manual of Useful Information* (1840), pp.5–17

Jeffreys' trial: *Authentick Memoirs of the Wicked Life and Transactions of Elizabeth Jeffreys, Spinster* (1754); *Authentick Tryals of John Swan and Elizabeth Jeffreys* (1752). Vestiges, August–November 1970, Vestry House Museum. Policing: Clarke, *The History*, pp.50–1. Whipps Cross: Walter A. Locks, *East London Antiquities* (London, 1902), p.137

Commons: Clarke, *The History*, p.12; Todd, *Vestry Minutes* (1926), p.46; Lysons, *The Environs*, p.204

William Dilwyn Diaries (transcribed by Richard Morris, University of Swansea), 20 January 1783, 10 May 1785

'Memoirs of Joel Johnson' W199 WFALSL; Hanson in Arthur Young, *Annals of Agriculture* (1802), pp.145–6; Burrell at House of Commons Select Committee on Smithfield Market 1847, Minutes of Evidence, pp.211–5

Hay: William Gaspey, *Tallis's Illustrated London* (London, 1851), p.231, *Chelmsford Chronicle*, 21 January 1876; *John Bull*, 22 June 1846

Enclosures: TNA MAF 1/682; *Lloyd's Weekly*, 30 January 1848

Population change: Clarke, *The History*, p.43

Brick-making: John Rocque's map Barns, *Vestry Minutes* (1925), p.18; Wragg Biography File WFALSL

Mills: KR Fairclough, 'Mills and Ferries Along The Lower Lea' in *Essex Archaeology and History*, 23 (1992), pp.61–2; Copper Mill Buildings File WFALSL; LMA ACC/2558/EL/A/33/010, ACC/2558/MW/C/15/288/3, ACC/2558/MW/C/15/288/4,5; ACC/2558/MW/C/15/288/003, the *Birmingham Journal*, 16 July 1859. *Liverpool Mercury*, 19 November 1824

Sweeps: Society for the Superseding of the Necessity of Climbing Boys (1816), pp.10–28; James Montgomery, *The Chimney Sweeper's Friend* (1824), pp.208–13; The Repertory of Arts, Manufactures and Agriculture (1803), p.159; Committee on Employment of Boys in Sweeping Chimnies, House of Commons (23 June 1817)

Anti-slavery: David Barclay, *An Account of the Emancipation of the Slaves of Unity Valley Pen in Jamaica* (1812); *The Anti-Slavery Reporter*, 1 November 1855

Chartism: *The Reformer's Year-book 1867*, pp.19–21; *Memories* (London, 1895), pp.34–77; *The Charter*, 28 April 1839; TNA HO 65/13; Linton; W.J. Linton

Ebenezer Clarke in J. Newton-Nind, *Mary Clarke Nind and Her Life and Work* (Chicago, 1906), pp.1–11; *Anti-Slavery Reporter*, 10 February 1862; Corn laws: *Bell's New Weekly Messenger*, 5 September 1841; *Morning Advertiser*, 28 December 1841; church rates ERO Q/SBb 540/30/1, 2; *Essex Standard*, 3 July 1840

Schools: Clarke, *The History*, pp.23–26; Morris, see John William McKail, *The Life of William Morris Volume 1* (London, 1901), pp.2–25

7 Land Societies, Philanthropy and Reform in the Railway Age

Freehold land societies: *The Freeholder*, 1 February, 1 May, 1 June, 1 July, 1 October, 2 December 1850; Whittingham Biography file WFALSL; Harold Bellman, *Bricks and Mortals* (London, 1949), pp.34–9

The Freeholder's Circular, 1 March 1852, 1 January, 1 November 1853; 2 October 1854; *The Freehold Land Times*, 1, 15 June, 15 August, 1 September 1854; *The Land and Building News*, 1 March 1855

Tower Hamlets estate at *The Freehold Land Times*, 1, 15 June, 15 August 1854

Mantz: *Northern Star and Leeds General Advertiser*, 16 December 1843; 16 March 1844; *Freehold Land Times*, 1 September 1854; Clarke, *The History*, pp.45–66. Court case, Old Bailey Proceedings Online (www.oldbaileyonline.org, version 7.2, 24 September 2017), April 1858, trial of ALFRED LONDON (t18580405-456)

Voters: Clarke, *The History*, p.46; Vestry meeting, *Stratford Times*, 5 May 1858

Old customs: William Houghton, *Walthamstow: Its Highways and Byways* (Walthamstow Antiquarian Society, 1937), p.24; Gilbert Houghton, *Walthamstow Past and Present* (Walthamstow, 1929), pp.14–15

Clarke's cottages: *Chelmsford Chronicle* 29 August 1862, the *Stratford Times*, 12 August 1859; *Journal of the Statistical Society*, Vol. 8, 1875, p.57; Clarke, *Chelmsford Chronicle*, 29 August 1862; *Morning Post*, 26 December 1862, Ebenezer Clarke, *The Hovel and The Home* (London, 1870), pp.9–35

Philanthropy: *The Stratford Times*, 12 August 1859; H.E. Hunt and Ambrose Barker, *Fifty Years A Club* (Walthamstow Working Men's Club, 1913), pp.10–17. Railways: Houghton, *Walthamstow* (1929), p.9; *Clerkenwell News* 9, 11 October 1869; TNA MT 6/66/11; Lammas rights *Chelmsford Chronicle*, 17 April 1840

8 Railway Suburb: Builders, Terraces and Timetables

Line Opening: *Tottenham and Edmonton Herald*, 7 May 1870; *Lloyd's Weekly Newspaper*, 1 May 1870; *Walthamstow Chronicle*, 6 July 1872; Great Eastern Railway Timetables, 1870, 1872 Nineteenth Century Collections Online; *Essex Newsman*, 28 May 1870; Houghton, *Walthamstow* (1929), p.35

Hoe Street station: Hatley, *Across the Years*, pp.11–45; *Walthamstow Chronicle*, 26 September 1874

Great Eastern Railway Timetables, 1874, Nineteenth Century Collections Online, p.50; British workman, *Walthamstow Guardian*, 10 February 1877

Housing: Report from the Select Committee Report on Artizans' and Labourers' Dwellings, 1882 pp.89–90; Jesse Argyle, 'Walthamstow' in *Life and Labour of the People in London* (London, 1902), pp.258–9

Tower hamlets: *The Builder*, 3 January 1874; *Walthamstow Chronicle*, 21 Feb, 16 May 1874; Speculative builders *Walthamstow Whip* 18, 25 September 1897; Argyle, 'Walthamstow', p.255

Jerry-building: *Walthamstow Whip*, 18 September 1897; LBM 27 April 1887; *Walthamstow Guardian*, 6 November 1880; Editorial in *Walthamstow Express*, 20 August 1887

Edward Good: *Walthamstow Guardian*, 21, 28 April 1922 WG; *The District Times*, 15 November 1901

Brickfields: 'Memories of an Old Chapel Ender, S.J. Smith', Moon's Farm Building File, WFALSL; *Walthamstow Guardian* 21, 28 April 1883

Terraces: Ordnance Survey 1865 map. Rural areas *Walthamstow Chronicle*, 6, 8 January 1876; The Official Guide to the Great Eastern Railway (London, 1892), pp.60–1

Cedars: *Walthamstow Guardian* 9 December 1882, 27 January 1883; George Bosworth, *More Walthamstow Houses* (Walthamstow Antiquarian Society, 1933), p.18

Morris: Clive Wilmer (ed.), *News from Nowhere and Other Writings* (London, 2004), p.415; Mackail, *William Morris*, p.4

Warner's estate: Local Board Minutes 4 November 1887 WFALSL; ERO D/DXj20, and background at Philip Plummer and Walter Bowyer, *A Brief History of Courtenay Warner and Warner Estate* (Walthamstow Historical Society, 2000). Warner's political career ERO D/DXj 20

Schools: *History of the Walthamstow School Board*, pp.15–16; George Bosworth, *The Borough Guide to Walthamstow* (1939), p.10

Methodist: H.B. Kendall, *The Origin and History of the Primitive Methodist Church*, pp.507–8; LMA ACC/1926/G/001

Salvation Army: *The Foundation of the Past* (1988, Salvation Army International Heritage Centre), *The War Cry*, 24 November 1888; Pubs at *Behind the Bar*, Waltham Forest Oral History Workshop, pp.20–1

Frederick Best: Local Board Minutes 12 May 1876, 23 June 1876 WFALSL WF47.2/2; *Walthamstow Chronicle*, 9, 20 May 1876, 7, 21 October; 18 November 1876; Bosanquet, *Walthamstow Chronicle* 7 October 1876, 21 October 76 18 Nov 76

Nuisances Committee: Local Board Minutes 17 October, 3 November, 5 December 1873; 12 June, 10 July 1874; 11 February 1876

Sewage farms: *Walthamstow Chronicle* 10 January 1874; House of Commons Select Committee on Rivers Pollution (1886), pp.61–96

Population: A.D. Law, *The Streets*, p.10 Jesse Argyle, 'Walthamstow' in *Life and Labour of the People in London*, by Charles Booth, First Series (London, 1902), pp.254–71; Land value *Walthamstow Guardian*, 14 January 1882

9 Dormitory Town: Radicals, Clerks and Costermongers

Woods: *Manchester Guardian*, 4 February 1897; *Walthamstow Reporter*, 29 Jan, 5, 19 Feb 1897, 22 July 1898; *Walthamstow Whip*, 4, 6 February 1897; *Walthamstow Guardian*, 22 January 1897, 5 February 1897; John Shepherd, 'A Lancashire Miner in Walthamstow: Sam Woods and the By-Election of 1897' *Essex Journal* 1987 22/1, pp.11–14

District council: *Walthamstow Reporter*, 26 October, 21 December 1894, 11 January 1895, 2 April 1897; *Walthamstow Reporter and Gazette*, 4 March 1904; *Daily Graphic*, 4 November 1902; Urban District Council Minutes minutes, 23 April 1897 WFALSL; C.M. Lloyd, *Urban District Councils* (Fabian Society Tract 189, 1920), pp.3–7

SDF: *Walthamstow Herald*, 8 April, 23 September 1893; *Walthamstow Reporter*, 14 December 1894, 21 June 1895, 30 August, 6, 27 September 1901; *Walthamstow Reporter and Gazette*, 15 April 1904, 2 February, 23 March 1906; *Walthamstow Whip*, 13, February 20 March, 2 October 1897; *The Socialist Critic*, 21 April, March, 28 July 1900; 30 November 1900; Bowman, *Walthamstow Reporter*, 14 December 1894

Tories: *Walthamstow Reporter*, 19 February 1897; 8 November, 18 October 1 November 1901, 18 March 1898; *Walthamstow and Leyton Herald*, 2, 9 April 1898; *Walthamstow Reporter*

Jolly: *Walthamstow Guardian*, 7 February 1913; *St James's Illustrated Review*, 1906 WFALSL

Good: *Walthamstow Reporter*, 8 February 1895; 7 January 1898; *Walthamstow Guardian*, 28 April 1922; *The District Times*, 15 November 1901

SDF campaigns: *The Socialist Critic*, 25 August 1900; 27 October 1900; Labour, *Walthamstow Reporter and Gazette*, 2,3, 9 February, 9, 23 March, 6 April 1906, 15 March 1907; *Walthamstow Reporter and Gazette*, 18 March 1904; 13 April, 27 April 1906; 20 March, 10 April, 24 April, 29 May 1908; *The District Times* 1 December 1905

Lady Warwick: *Essex Newsman*, 25 February 1905; 14 September 1929

Osbourne: *The District Times*, 9 July 1909; unveiling 23 July 1909 24 December 1909 wins case; 2 September 1910

Suffragettes: *The District Times*, 19 July 1901, *The District Times*, 4 November 14 October 1910

Mutiny trial: *London Daily News*, 25 January 1909; TNA FO 371/136/283-295; *The District Times*, 15, 22 March 1912

Reservoirs: *The Daily Graphic*, 9 July 1901; *Walthamstow Reporter*, 1 January 1897; 14 January 1898

Building workers: UDC minutes, Highways Committee 8 July 1897; *Walthamstow Reporter*, 2 July 1897, 1 September 1898; Diary of Eli Rose, 13 July 1895 ACC 8662 WFALSL

Servants: *Essex Herald*, 18 February 1890, 8 February 1892; *Walthamstow Reporter*, 12 April 1895; Engineering: *The District Times*, 21 October 1910; Hatley, *Across the Years*, p46; Richard Fox, *Smoky Crusade* (London, 1938), pp.58–66

Trains: LMA LCC/CL/HSG/1/79;

Dormitory town: Hatley, *Across the Years*, p.62; Harry Greenstock, *Go On and Prosper: Reminiscences of the Early Day in the Plastics Industry* (London, 1981), pp.22–3; *The Daily Chronicle*, 21 March 1905

Variety: Eric Krieger Collection GB 3401 KRG; *Walthamstow Reporter*, 25 January, 15 November 1901

Rose leisure time: Eli Rose diary 7, 21 April; 6 October, 5 May, 1 August WFALSL

Bicycles: *Walthamstow Whip*, 22 May 1897; *Walthamstow Reporter*, 29 January 1897; 7, 15 April 1898; Cinemas, Guy Osbourne, Conservation Officer;

15 September 1997, Committee Report, Planning and Economic Development; Cinema, W38.5 WFALSL; Cart horse parade, *Walthamstow Reporter*, 11 January 1895

Grosvenor House: *Walthamstow Reporter*, 4 October 1895

Local history: *The District Times* 20 March, 8 May 1908; ERO T/P 75/1

High Street: Local Board Minutes 22 December 1882, 26 June 1885 *Walthamstow Guardian*, 17 April 1880; 3, 19 December 1884 WFALSL

Everett's model bakery: *Walthamstow Guardian*, 8 January 1897

Norwood: *Shillinglaw's Walthamstow Directory 1882*; 3 July 1882 W71 BC/1/1 Register of Deposited Plans, WFALSL

Warner's shops: Guy Osbourne, *Leucha Road Conservation Area* (London Borough of Waltham Forest)

Street stalls: *Walthamstow Reporter*, 1 November 1901; *The District Times*, 21 April 1905; Co-op; *Walthamstow Reporter*, 2 November 1894; Information provided by Co-operative Society Archives, Shop hours *The District Times* 17 May 1912

Great War: Alistair MacLellan, 'Anti-German Sentiment in Walthamstow August–September 1914', www.historyofsorts.wordpress.com 25 September 2016

10 The People's Century

Great War: Notes in Papers of Robert Barltop 5/1, Bishopsgate Institute; www.walthamstowwarmemorial.co.uk, War Memorials Register, Imperial War Museums; George Bosworth, *Walthamstow Official Guide* (1935), p.31 'Soldiers Died in the Great War 1914–1919 Part 48 The Essex Regiment (London, 1921), p.48; Zepplins: Alan Simpson, *Air Raids on South-West Essex in the Great War* (Barnsley, 2015), pp.90–136; TNA MH 47/96/44

Labour: *Essex Newsman* 9 November 1929, *Chelmsford Chronicle* 25 December 1925;

Housing: Law, *The Streets*, p.10; 'Memories of an Old Chapel Ender, S.J. Smith', Moon's Farm Building File, WFALSL; *The Borough of Walthamstow Official Guide* (1961), pp.59–61, TNA HLG 23/1261; TNA HLG 23/6246; TNA HLG 23/1258; TNA HLG 23/1062

Incorporation and pageant: George Bosworth, *Walthamstow: The Official Guide*, p11; *Western Times*, 23 July 1926; WBC Education Committee, Final Report on Historical Pageant W03.3 Walthamstow Pageant File WFALSL; George Roebuck, Book of the Walthamstow Pageant (Walthamstow Antiquarian Society, 1930), pp.24–5; *Walthamstow Guardian* 17 October 1930

Vestry house: Typescript notes. File on Walthamstow Boat, Haringey Archive Service and Local Studies Library

Lammas meadows: LMA ACC/2423/AL/080

Walthamstow stadium: Norman Jacobs, *Speedway in London* (Stroud, 2001), p.191; Miscellaneous articles, Walthamstow Stadium Buildings File WFALSL

Cinema: www.brind.co.uk/html/CINEMAS/60th.html; *The Sphere*, 10 December 1932, W38.5

Unemployed: *Chelmsford Chronicle*, 13 January 1933, *Chelmsford Chronicle*, 11 November 1932; Information on the Greek Theatre from Oona Kelly at Walthamstow School for Girls

Thomas Linehan, *East London for Mosley* (London, 1996), pp.115–21; Robert Barltrop Papers, Barltrop 5/1 Bishopsgate Institute

War: Mass Observation Online, Evacuation 1939–1944; Sixty Years of Progress' Fuller Electric, pp.20–2, W25.1; Ros Wyld, *The War Over Walthamstow: The Story of Civil Defence 1939–1945* (Walthamstow Borough Council 1945), pp.15–18; ASEA Electric Ltd ARP, 'Air Raid Precaution Scheme', ASEA File W25.1 WFALSL; Note on Inauguration 18 October 1997, Monoux Almshouses Buildings File, WFALSL

Post-war Walthamstow: *Daily Worker* 4 July 1945; *Daily Herald*, 4 July 1945; Priory Court Building File, WFALSL; *Walthamstow Forward*, No. 3, Vol. 1, June 1947; *Priory Court: Flats at Countess Road Walthamstow*, Cement and Concrete Association (1949) Guildhall Library, PAM 12172; 'Towards a Plan for Walthamstow', Reconstruction and Housing Committee, December 1946; Journal of the South-West Essex Technical College and School of Art, Vol. 3, No. 4, September 1953, pp.191–9; 'Our Town' Walthamstow 1951, Festival Souvenir Programme W03.3 WFALSL

Toy industry: Waltham Forest Oral History Workshop, Interviews with Jean Ralston and Sue Russell; Gary Heales, *Toys: A Serious Business*, Vestry House Museum W24.8; *Walthamstow Post*, 1 May 1958; *The Borough of Walthamstow Official Guide 1961*, pp.48–74

Factories: *Contact: The House Organ of Asea Electric Ltd*, Walthamstow, Vol. 8 1/2 January–February 1956; Vol. 8 3/4 March–April 1956, W25.1

Heritage: Marjorie Batsford, *Timber-Framed Buildings in Waltham Forest*, pp.6–18; Guy Osborne, *Walthamstow Village Conservation Area*, LBWF (2005); www.e17pumphouse.org.uk/History.html

Youth: Apprenticeship with ASEA' W25.1; Walthamstow Mercury and Post 16 October 1958; George Bosworth, *Walthamstow: The Official Guide* (1935), pp.30–1; Mass Observation Online Adult and Higher Education 1937–40; B. Cantes (ed.), *Walthamstow Road Users' Guide*, pp.13–21; Small wonder: Interview with Pete Stennett, Music Like Dirt blog, 22 July 2013, W25.3

Immigration and population: post-war guide W72.21 pamphlet 11 November 1959; 1971 Census: Demographic, Social and Economic Indices for Wards in Greater London WF31.1; Peter Ashan, *Remembering Slavery and its Legacy 1807–2007* (Waltham Forest Arts Council, 2007), pp.35–6

Deindustrialisation: *Waltham Forest Guardian*, 1 April 1988; *Yellow Advertiser*, 4 October 1991; *Gazette Newspapers*, 30 September 1983; Britains W24.8

About the Author

JAMES DIAMOND trained as a journalist and wrote for local newspapers in north London and worked as a sub-editor for national newspapers including *The Daily Mirror*. Since leaving the newspaper industry he has worked in local government in London as a press officer. He has an MA in Economic and Social History. He lives in Walthamstow in one of the houses built by the old Warner estate company.

Index

Printed in Great Britain
by Amazon